"Rabbi John Carrier's] in this compelling book. This is for anyone who has struggled with the big questions of life, and isn't that all of us? Dive in and connect!"

— Rabbi Rebecca W. Sirbu,
Director for Rabbis Without Borders

"Whether you are Jewish or not, Rabbi Carrier's teachings encourage you to live your life to your full potential. His methods have helped me immensely in my spiritual and personal life. A must-read for those seeking spiritual growth."

— Kevin McIntyre,
Photographer

"I devoured this exceptional book in one sitting! The tone and gentle humor of Rabbi Carrier's writing is perfect. His bravery in uncovering less-than-good parts of his earlier life is so appreciated. We all struggle. Most importantly, he made the Jewish faith so attractive; it is even tempting for this 64-year-old Christian woman!"

— Marilyn Grunwald,
Writer & Consultant

"Written with humor by someone who has searched for his own promised life, this book is a wonderful step-by-step guide to start you on your own journey. Great advice for anyone, Jewish or not. As John Carrier says, you don't have to do it all at once. Take each step as you are ready with the confidence that he's there to help you."

— Liam Woodfin,
Retail Sales Associate

"I already feel the power of Rabbi Carrier's words serving as both inspiration and motivation in my ongoing journey of self-reflection and self-discovery. I believe that when you read The Promised Life you, too, will feel that empowerment and the desire to apply his thoughts and ideas your daily life."

— Hilary Steinberg,
Early Childhood Educator

"Culturally I was taught to only accept advice from elders. Extrapolating this, it would seem accepting advice from a 3,500-year-old way of life is even better! My interest in Judaism is what made me pick up the book. Rabbi Carrier's easy-going prose is what kept me with it till the end."

— Hammad Ali,
Graduate Student in Computer Science

THE
PROMISED
LIFE

THE PROMISED LIFE

Overcome Your Crisis and Find Your Purpose with Seven Gifts from a Time-Tested Tradition

BY JOHN CARRIER

Published by Author Academy Elite
P.O. Box 43, Powell, OH 43035
www.AuthorAcademyElite.com

Paperback ISBN: 978-1-64085-189-4

Hardcover ISBN: 978-1-64085-190-0

Library of Congress Control Number: 2017919771

Illustrations by Kara Carrier
firebirdvisuals.com

Cover Design by Aleksandar Petrović
alehandropetrovic.com

Author Photographs by Kevin McIntyre
kevinmcphotograph.com

Dedicated to my family:
My sons, who got me on the path;
My daughters, who inspire me to stay there; and
My wife, the wind at my back and my
constant companion.

"Do not oppress the stranger, and you know the heart of the stranger, for you were strangers in the land of Egypt."

— Exodus 23:9

TABLE OF CONTENTS

INTRODUCTION
THE PROMISE

"Every descent is for the sake of ascent."
— Hassidic saying

"We can easily forgive a child who is afraid of the dark; the real tragedy of life is when adults are afraid of the light."
— Plato

Who You Are

We don't know each other, but I hope that's about to change.

If you found this book, I'm guessing you have some computer savvy and the wherewithal to own an electronic device on which to read it. You're not a trash-picking landfill-gleaner in Calcutta (no judgments of those who are). You're not reading this in a mosquito-netted bed in sub-Saharan Africa, beginning to feel the fever set in as a near-victim of the Ebola virus, God forbid. You are more likely a fully-enfranchised citizen of a wealthy nation, most likely the United States, and you have (statistically speaking) all of your adult teeth. You may not know what your next meal is — so many choices! — but you know with certainty that there will be one. These and other factors put you in the top 1 percent of the most fortunate human beings on Earth.

And yet . . . you suffer.

While people may share their own opinions as to the relative "merit" of your suffering over the suffering of others, my sense is that you feel it no less acutely. The sensations of suffering come from the same soup of hormones and neurotransmitters whether you're:

- dying of a curable disease in a degenerate hospital in the tropics;
- hiding from the secret police in central Asia or the theocratic brute squads of the Middle East;
- or swallowing the bile that rises when you see your work cubicle on a Tuesday morning after a holiday weekend, whether or not there is a picture of your beloved family or bitchin' Camaro pinned to the fabric wall or magnetized to the whiteboard.

In economics and finance (my first career) there is a theory: There's no such thing as a valid interpersonal utility comparison. In English: You can't count other people's money, and if someone tells me they are suffering, I have no right nor basis to argue with them that they are not.

Different kitchen maybe, but it's the same soup.

What I can tell you from my own experience — growing up relatively privileged in what has been, at least from the day of my birth until the time of this writing, the wealthiest country in the history of countries, and yet personally struggling for decades with occasional waves of deep depression, financial insecurity, relationships both awesome and terrible, successes both durable and meaningless, and periodic suicidal ideation — is this: Our suffering, friend, usually comes from the same place: It is existential.

We inherit identities. We are born in countries and inherit citizenship. We are born into families (or are adopted by them), and without trying too hard, or having much of a say in the matter, we inherit ethnic peoplehood and even religious practices. There was a time when most people also inherited their livelihood or career. If you were born a boy, you did what your dad did — whether he was a farmer, a blacksmith, or a rabbi. If you were born a girl, you became a mother and a housewife like your own mother; in some parts of the world, this is still the case.

Enter a thoroughly modern affliction: Having been taught that we can make decisions about our life based on our own satisfaction or lack thereof, we now suffer when we experience no satisfaction from our inherited identities, whether this suffering is because we fail to meet the expectations of that identity, or — and this can be worse — when we succeed completely in that identity and still feel empty inside. This has been true for some time in relation to career choices, when industrialization and urbanization over the last couple of centuries made career choices even possible. But now, uniquely within our time and place in history we can trade our inherited identities for acquired or constructed ones. And now, more than ever, one aspect of interchangeable identity is the choice we get to make about our religious practice and what religious community we choose to belong to (if any).

According to the report "America's Changing Religious Landscape" by the Pew Research Center, one-third of American adults no longer practices the religion of their upbringing, whether they swap it for a new one, or they drop out of religion altogether. Historically speaking, this has never happened before; most people were born, lived, and died in the religion and culture of their birth parents for most of the history of the world. But whether we trade up or drop out, we try again to experience a purpose to our existence, and whether we succeed or fail to find that life of purpose, we continue to suffer.

And that's real. The hurt is real. Without the experience of personal significance, of meaning, of joy, of personal growth, without the ability to connect with other human beings over some shared purpose or value, the impulse to self-destruct (more likely: self-medicate) is real.

Look, if none of this resonates with you, God bless you. I'm grateful that the Source of All Blessing has blessed you with understanding and peace. In that case I ask you for a favor: Read a little bit further, or even to the end (it's not a long book), just in case you see something useful for a friend of yours who suffers and might be helped if you pass this book along to them. I'd be much obliged.

But if you have felt a glimmer of recognition in anything I've written so far, if you feel like I know you and know your struggle even a little bit, I want to give you a gift. It's only fair that you get to know me a little bit, too, and once we know each other better, I want to share with you one path out of the deep, dark woods. Now, I only know one path for sure, the one that I've taken, and the one that many of my friends and students have taken with life-changing results, and that path may not be for everyone, including you. Nevertheless, this is one path I feel I can speak about with some authority, though I humbly acknowledge that all advice is, ultimately, autobiography. Your mileage may vary.

Who I Am

In my tradition, the relationship between a teacher and a student is an important one — sacred, even — and critical to that relationship is our mutual understanding where each of us is coming from, in order to establish trust for the important work ahead.

Personally, I'm coming from quite a long way away.

Today I'm an ordained rabbi, trained in the Conservative/Masorti denomination of Judaism, but I was not born Jewish. In fact, my father was a third-generation Southern Baptist minister. Of course, by the time I was born, he had retired to begin his second career as a college professor. We lived in a small town in East Texas called Commerce. Few people have heard of Commerce, outside of the rodeo circuit. My mom was also a teacher, and both my parents ignited in me a passion for learning and sharing that learning with others.

When I was 10 years old, we moved to southern West Virginia for my father's work, and I spent many formative years in the communities of Appalachia. A different brand of Southern hospitality, more hillbilly than redneck (I can say that about my people), and different accents, but it reinforced for me the importance of hospitality all the same, the importance of meeting people where they are and accepting how they are, and the inherent dignity of all people, even those outside of the cultural mainstream. As much I am now a Yankee living in sunny Southern California, I get equally homesick reading J.D. Vance's book *Hillbilly Elegy* and watching Mike Judge's TV show *King of the Hill*. Something about that decorative clock made out driftwood in the shape of Texas, hanging in Hank Hill's cartoon kitchen, always makes me think of my Aunt Susie and Uncle Ernie's house, may their memory be a blessing.

As a youth, I haunted the local college library, where I once found a guide to private high schools in New England. I caught hold of a crazy scheme to escape the hollows, and I begged my parents to send me to boarding school. Between my parents' chief value of education and the struggling public school system of West Virginia, they acquiesced. I went to high school in Connecticut and college in Baltimore. In Baltimore, I dated a Jewish girl for the first time, and within a couple of years we were married, and within a couple of years more, we had two sons. Then, in my quest to be the best father I could be to boys being raised in their mother's tradition, coupled with my desire to find answers to questions that began to burn within me, I became Jewish myself. Not because I had to in order to get married, but because over the years I grew to love the Jewish traditions, wisdom, and people as much as I loved the particular Jewish people in my family. By this point we lived in Virginia, just outside Washington, D.C., near my in-laws.

Shortly thereafter we moved to Knoxville, Tennessee, and I was at once back in Appalachia (in the foothills of the Great Smoky Mountains), and at the same time, immersed in the Jewish practice of a small but enduring community that was a mix of recent immigrants from Europe and the Lower East Side of Manhattan, along with Southern Jews of the old school. The latter's families had come west with the mercantile expansion of the

United States and had been settled in the Smokies for over a hundred years. We came to Knoxville (Go Vols!) for my wife to attend graduate school. After two years, she transferred to another program in Minneapolis, Minnesota (Go Gophers!).

As I'd learned in Knoxville, one of the quickest and easiest ways for a Jewish person or family to integrate into a new community was to join a synagogue; doubtless this is true for any religious person, but we Jews have, for better or worse, perfected the art of resettling after displacement. As it happened, we'd bought a house across the street from a synagogue, without even knowing it was there. I also found out that, just as a synagogue can be vital for a family to retain stability while in transit, so to can it be critical for an individual in transition. A year after we moved to Minneapolis, my wife and I separated. Of course, I could no longer bear to show up for daily prayers in a building within sight of a house that was no longer my home. Nevertheless, just as I was feeling most unmoored from all things familiar and safe, it was a friend from another synagogue, named Sid, who extended a hand: He invited me to join his family for Passover, the Jewish holiday most closely associated with the home life of a Jewish family. I was still lonely, but I was no longer alone. For all its wonder and reputation, Southern hospitality barely holds a candle to the way Jews welcome the stranger. From the day Abraham welcomed three strangers out of the heat and into his tent (Genesis 18), to the day Sid brought me in from the cold, we have gone out of our way to ease the path and support the journey of wandering souls and seekers like me and you.

After the end of my marriage, and during the hard time that followed — a time of loneliness, financial struggle, dissatisfaction with my career — I had begun to spend more and more time at the synagogue (Sid's). And things got better. A couple of years later, part of that additional time at the synagogue became occupied by classes on Judaism that I was attending with my new bride-to-be, who had decided to convert to Judaism before we got married. Around the same time, I had begun to re-evaluate my work as a consultant in finance and computer systems, seeking a way to make a bigger impact on the world and to be part of a cause much greater than myself. Then it hit me out of the blue: What if I could take the traditions and learning that had so transformed me, and move them from the periphery of my life to the center . . . by changing careers to become a teacher of those traditions? Wouldn't that be *enough* of a life of service? Could I think of a cause outside myself than was bigger than serving an entire people, while serving God? Besides, in a way, I'd be returning to the family business: a fourth-generation preacher, albeit in a different franchise.

One year of intense conversations with my rabbi and five years of seminary later, I was ordained as a *Rav B'Yisrael* — a master teacher among the people Israel, a rabbi. And not for nothing: *Yisrael* is a Hebrew name that first appears in the Bible (Genesis 32:22-32) when Jacob, one of the patriarchs of the Jewish people, is on a mission to return to his homeland and face his estranged brother Esau, after years of running from his own past. On the way, he encountered a mysterious figure on the banks of the river Jabbok — some say an angel, some say a demon, some say his own brother — and spent the entire night wrestling with him. Before dawn broke, the fleeing figure blessed Jacob and gave him his second name: *Yisrael*. It means, "One who struggles with beings both human and divine, and yet prevails." My ordination recognized me, the son of a preacher turned professor, myself a redneck turned hillbilly turned boarding school brat, a baptized Christian turned intellectual atheist turned religious Jew, from Texas, West Virginia, Connecticut, Maryland, Virginia, Tennessee, Minnesota, and California (with short stints in New York City and Jerusalem), as a master teacher of the tradition of a people that has endured 4,000 years of being kicked out of every country in the developed world, and yet has prevailed. Their story is my story, a story of crisis, of revelation of great gifts, and of ultimate purpose.

Soon after ordination, I took a position as the rabbi of a wonderful congregation in Southern California. True, seminary taught me a lot of sacred text and the history and mechanics of our traditions and rituals, but when it came time for me to lead, teach, inspire, challenge, and pastor to this people, I had to learn that from scratch. As of this writing, that was about four years ago. My congregation has been patient with me as I grew into my role here, they have inspired me to continue my growth, and they have taught me the Torah of the human heart — as important as, and inseparable from, the Torah God gave to Moses on Mount Sinai. Man, I thought I knew some stuff before; I had no idea.

But I've learned. I've learned that the Jewish people have been blessed with great gifts, and these gifts, though they first came to light in stories of divine revelation about 3,000 years ago, have carried and sustained this most durable and audacious people from that day to this. These very gifts, though ancient in origin, are the most effective means I have seen — and I've seen a lot — for facing and prevailing against the most difficult challenges of modern life: fear, anger, loneliness, boredom, anxiety, depression, need, want, and the feeling of purposelessness. Further, I've learned that these gifts were given to the Jewish people not to hoard and hide as a treasure for us alone, but to bless the world with them by sharing them. These gifts are not only shareable and teachable; they are effective, I believe, for anyone who would accept and use them, regardless of their spiritual or cultural background, for thriving and flourishing in a world filled with challenges we all face.

What I Believe

Who I am and the journey I've traveled have led me to believe the following in my heart of hearts:

- Everyone, everywhere has the ability and the right to grow.
- Everyone, everywhere desires the experience of living a meaningful life.
- Everyone, everywhere desires the experience of joy.
- Everyone, everywhere benefits from greater human connection.
- The Torah and the Jewish traditions that have evolved from it (and continue to evolve from it) provide robust, resilient, and enduring principles for human connection, joy, meaning, and personal and communal growth. Furthermore, the Torah and these principles are available to everyone, everywhere.

Really? Everyone? Everywhere?
Yes, really.
Everyone.
Everywhere.
It is my informed opinion that the Torah was never meant to be kept in secret and sequestration by the Jewish people alone. Some rabbis and many Jews disagree with me about this; nevertheless, it's in the text itself, over

and over again, that the Torah, its related prophecies, wisdom literature, and subsequent commentaries had always been intended both for the enlightenment of the Jewish people AND for the betterment of all people who encounter this fountain of wisdom and blessing. When God made a deal with Abraham — a covenantal partnership, I should say — God told Abraham that he would not only be blessed himself, but also that he would be the source of blessing for those who encountered him, whether they were related to him or not. To this day, Jews are enjoined to be a light unto all the nations. (Isaiah 42:6)

This is true whether you believe that the Torah was given at a certain time and place to all the Jews of the world simultaneously (according to the story in Exodus about the revelation at Mount Sinai) or that the Torah as we know it today emerged over time as a bundle of scrolls which distilled much older oral traditions of the Hebrew people and were later knit together into a coherent whole (according to the latest academic theories).

Further, my teacher Rabbi Elliot Dorff explained to us that Judaism is an exoteric religion, rather than an esoteric one. What's the difference? Esoteric religions, by their nature and design, keep secrets. Many religions possess reverence for certain unknowable mysteries; particularly, in esoteric religions there are bodies of knowledge that are concealed from the general population who practice that religion, and this knowledge is revealed only to initiates, priests, or a similar inner cadre of practitioners.

In exoteric religions, by contrast, all sacred knowledge is available and open to study by all practitioners of that religion. The Torah is called the birthright or inheritance of the entire Jewish people, and converts to Judaism are regarded as equal in every way to Jews who were born Jewish. For us — that is, we converts — the Torah becomes our birthright and inheritance as well. You don't have to be a rabbi to study the Torah; all the honorific "rabbi" means is that someone has already studied enough to be certified as a trustworthy teacher of the Torah and traditions, at least by the standard of the people who ordain her or him. But any Jew can study the text . . . and not just Jews.

Our sacred literature cites many examples of sharing this wisdom with those who are perhaps not committed, but merely curious. Exodus describes the scene of the Hebrews' departure from Egypt being accompanied by a mixed multitude — both the descendants of Abraham as well as Egyptians and others who thought that the Hebrews were onto something, something that afforded a better life than could be promised by the Pharaoh and by Egyptian culture. Furthermore, a few weeks later, when these folks made it to the foot of Mount Sinai, *all* of them were present when God spoke the first Ten Utterances (commonly called the Ten Commandments). It wasn't like only Jews could hear God's voice, or that the mixed multitude were asked to wait in the bar while only Israelites got a seat at the table. Another of our holy texts, the Talmud, is full of stories about rabbis teaching non-Jews, and while some of those non-Jews decided to join the Jewish people because what they learned was so compelling (I did), Jewishness itself was never a prerequisite to study.

That said, there are a few sects of fundamentalists within Judaism who only teach certain curricula to Jews alone. This is especially true of the traditional oral transmission of Kabbalah (Jewish mysticism — the name itself means "transmission"), but as we've seen over the last couple of decades in Los Angeles, even that has been opened to non-Jews, especially but not exclusively if they are celebrities, and the books themselves that capture Kabbalistic teachings are able to be acquired and read by anyone. Like any major religion, Judaism has chauvinistic sub-groups that claim all Jewish knowledge and traditions as "our thing." Every religion has its fundamentalists, and we're no different.

But I am not one of them.

Why I Wrote This Book

I know I am not you, and your suffering is not my suffering; however, if you've made it this far, I'm willing to bet you and I have some shared experiences, some pain in common. That's where we come to my single favorite verse in the whole Torah:

> "You shall not oppress the stranger, and you know the heart of the stranger, because you were strangers in the land of Egypt."
> — Exodus 23:9

If you currently feel the kind of suffering I've described, I take it as a religious obligation (and a considerable honor) to do what I can to help, by sharing what I have learned in order to cope with it and ultimately rise above it. Furthermore, I've had so much help along the way — rabbis, teachers, fellow Jews, even my non-Jewish parents and relatives who supported me in doing something to improve the quality of my life and well-being — that I owe it to them to honor their investment in me by doing everything I can to teach anyone and everyone whose life I could help improve, including yours.

I wrote this book because I know the heart of the stranger, because I've been there, and now that others have welcomed me home, it's time for me to pay it forward. I will be the first to admit that this book and what it teaches is not for everyone. Nevertheless, it just might be for you.

How to Use This Book

This first part of the book has been about our getting to know each other, or at least you getting to know me. I make no assumptions about who you are or where you are coming from, but for the purposes of our learning together, I am willing to trust the following about you: I trust that you are an open-minded person, and I trust that you are self-aware enough to recognize that you would like to grow, and would appreciate a life of greater meaning. I trust that you are intelligent and have some degree of control over how you spend your time, even though your life may often make you feel otherwise. I trust that you are strong, and you are as prepared as you need to be for the journey; perhaps you're just looking for the trailhead.

What follows in the next section are the seven Jewish Gifts that I've found to be invaluable in my life. Once more, advice is only autobiography, and your experience be better or worse than (or just different from) mine. But judging from not only my experiences but also the experiences of my students, teachers, and friends, these Gifts are seven practices or categories of practice, any of which could dramatically improve the quality of your life and your experience of well-being, and taken together could form a new operating system, a new architecture, that opens you up to a life of growth, meaning, joy, and connection. These gifts are:

- **The Gift of Learning** – Taking time to grow your understanding every day.

- **The Gift of Gratitude** – Growing your satisfaction by giving thanks to the Source of your blessings.
- **The Gift of Distinction** – Exercising caution to take in only what serves you and to share only what serves all.
- **The Gift of Community** – Building stronger relationships and communities to nurture and support you.
- **The Gift of Inner Work** – Refining yourself by forgiving others, owning your weaknesses, and improving your habits.
- **The Gift of Outer Work** – Being sensitive to others' needs and taking responsibility for how you can help.
- **The Gift of Rest** – Pausing to love the world and yourself as-is, so you can recharge to face the important work of your life.

The chapters unwrapping these Seven Gifts each contain five parts:

- **Where You Are** – A description of the challenges you may be facing, which this Gift can help you overcome.
- **Where You Are Going** – A vision of your life when you open this Gift and undertake to master it.
- **Where It Comes From** – The source of this Gift in Jewish sacred texts and traditions.
- **Where I Am** – What this Gift has done for me personally in facing and overcoming my own challenges.
- **What to Do** – Five real, concrete actions you can take to begin using this Gift to improve your life and help you flourish today, regardless of who you are or where you come from.

How you approach the Seven Gifts is up to you. You may want to read through them quickly and then decide which one you want to focus on first, based on what is most interesting to you personally or what you think you need in your life most, right now. Or you may prefer to go step-by-step, trying the unwrap and implement the first gift first, second gift second, and so on. I have arranged them in a certain order intentionally, based on how I think they can best build on one another.

What I do not necessarily recommend is that you try to master all of the Gifts at once. I do not recommend this because, as smart and dedicated to growth as you are, taking it all on at once is probably counterproductive. I've been working on all of these areas for nearly 20 years, have experienced tremendous benefit from them, and have been deemed qualified to teach them by my own teachers and my community. Yet personally I still feel like I'm at the "advanced beginner" stage.

By way of example: When students of mine become interested in taking on the spiritual discipline of the Jewish dietary laws, or the portfolio of restrictions that come with a traditional observance of the Sabbath day, I always caution them to start slow, adopting one new ritual or rule at a time, because in my experience, when someone tries to take on all the rules and features at once, they are likely to become overwhelmed and burnt out by the experience, and they give up doing it, thus losing the profound benefits that come even with baby steps.

Look, you do you, but this is my advice: Start with one, and start slow. Fast will come soon enough, and better that you be ready for it, and warmed up so you don't pull something.

An important note: My goal in introducing you to the Seven Gifts is not to convince you or anyone else to convert to Judaism. You may be Jewish already (*mazal tov!*) and want to have a better understanding of your birthright. You may have already chosen the path to convert to Judaism. You may be simply "Jew-curious," or you may just be looking for tips and tricks and hacks to improve your life, with no interest in Judaism or religion or God or any of that stuff. My goal is to give you a useful guide to life-changing Gifts that I believe can help you meet your goals, regardless of where you are coming from. If it happens that you are curious, or become curious, about the process of becoming a full-fledged member of the Jewish people, know that I have included some information in the last chapter of this book to walk you through that process, if that it is your goal. It is not my goal that you convert, but I'd be honored if this book helps ease your path, if that's the path you choose for yourself.

Seeker, friend, thank you for taking this journey with me. Thank you for your trust. It is my great joy to be able to honor my own teachers and share what I've learned with you. I'm excited for us to learn together, and I can't wait to get started!

My Promise to You

In writing this book and putting it into your hands, I am making you a promise. Actually, I'm making you three promises:

- I promise you to teach you the very best of what I know to help you experience personal growth, meaning in your life, joy in your life, and greater human connection.
- I promise you to make that teaching as accessible and effective as I can for you, regardless of your background or religion (if any).

- I promise you that if you read this book, try out the recommended actions, and reach out to me or another teacher if you get stuck, you will notice change in your life. That change may be uncomfortable or painful at times. Growth is often uncomfortable; ask any teenager or pregnant person. But if you take this journey with me — with an open mind and an open heart — you will experience real growth in wonderful and perhaps unexpected ways.

It's a pleasure and an honor to be on this journey with you. One more gift before we start, not from the Jewish tradition, necessarily, but more from just me to you: I've created, and will continue to create, additional resources to complement and supplement each chapter in this book. I have also reserved a space for you to connect with me and with others who are reading this book and putting these gifts to work for them. To join this "Promised Life Tribe" and access a growing library of additional resources, please visit *www.promisedlifetribe.com* to learn more and connect with us.

Now . . . Let's get started.

THE FIRST GIFT
LEARNING

"Rabbi Tarfon and the Elders were once reclining in the upper story of Nitza's house, in Lod, when this question was posed to them: Which is greater, study or action? Rabbi Tarfon answered, saying: Action is greater. Rabbi Akiva answered, saying: Study is greater. All the rest agreed with Akiva that study is greater than action because it leads to action."

— *Kiddushin* 40b

"There is no end to education. It is not that you read a book, pass an examination, and finish with education. The whole of life, from the moment you are born to the moment you die, is a process of learning."

— Jiddu Krishnamurti

It is a gift to learn something every day, whether ancient traditions or new discoveries. Learning — that is, setting aside time every day for focused study — is the keystone Gift, not only because it informs and enables you to unwrap all other Gifts and opens and broadens your mind, but also because it gives you a sense of tangible progress and accomplishment as you complete and master texts and subjects that are important to you.

Where You Are

At some time in your life, you have been lost. I don't mean in the existential sense (there's that, too, and we'll get to that in a bit); I mean in the literal sense of winding up someplace you didn't expect with no clear direction on how to find your way out or reach the destination you set out to find. Maybe you were on a road trip, or in a corn maze or hedge labyrinth, in a fun house (often a misnomer!), or on your way to a party at a friend's house you've never been to before. You may have been lost in the woods on a weekend hike, or you may have been lost in a department store or an amusement park as a child, not knowing where your parent was. Nothing looks familiar, until such time as you wind up going in circles, and you keep passing the same landmarks with increasing frustration. You're in foreign territory; you feel like a stranger. Perhaps that is why many people hesitate to stop and ask for directions: The worst sensations of being lost are admitting that you are lost, feeling like you don't belong where you are, and exposing yourself as a foreigner or an ignoramus to someone who might be able to help you.

In a state of feeling existentially lost — i.e. not knowing your role or purpose in life, not knowing which direction to take, feeling like a foreigner not only in your own land, but in your own skin — the immediate physical dangers like running out of gas in a remote area or accidentally driving off a cliff, are much less severe, but the feelings of frustration compound tenfold. More than that: When you are existentially lost, asking for directions is harder.

First, if you're looking for a particular place in physical space, like a friend's house or the nearest gas station, there's only one location for everyone, and any person who knows the area can help you. If you're looking for the purpose of your life, your destination may be different from everyone else who might be on the same path. In this latter kind of confusion, you may be embarrassed to ask for directions, especially if you think everyone else already has it figured out and is riding on cruise control to a known location.

Spoiler alert: We don't, and we're not.

Second, in this kind of being lost, there's no shortage of people who are willing to give you directions to the place *they* think you should go, and they may tell you whether you ask or not.

But maybe you're not lost. Maybe you are exactly where you should be, or you're on the path that makes the most sense, yet you feel like you don't belong. You feel like a foreigner in a place where you should feel at home, all the more insecure because it seems like everyone around you speaks the language and knows the customs, but you don't. This could be at work, or at home, or at social settings with your peers. Everyone seems to get the joke but you, so you must not have the right background or knowledge to get the joke, or it must be in a language you don't fully understand.

By way of example, many rabbis I know who serve synagogues decry the fact that most of the members of the community don't attend regular prayer services most of the time. I hear from clergy of all faiths and denominations: It's not just rabbis who notice this. In our case, I don't believe it's out of lack of commitment to Judaism; these non-attendees take great pride in their Jewish identity and they contribute to community with volunteer labor and financial donations. My hypothesis is that a couple of generations' removal from socially enforced daily practice, the common knowledge of the service has waned. See, back in the ghettos — segregated Jewish neighborhoods of European cities — or rural villages, there was nothing else happening in town when prayer services were happening, and everybody noticed if you skipped, so there was a cultural expectation of attendance. Now, when committed Jews enter the prayer space of their synagogue, they feel like they are walking into a foreign embassy on native soil, where everyone is speaking another language, which everyone else understands. The tragedy is that the synagogue is the one place where every Jew should feel at home, anywhere in the world, where they automatically fit in, where they should feel safer than anywhere else. However, because of the decline of regular learning and practice, the single most safe place, everyone's last refuge, feels foreign and unsafe, so people avoid it like the bad part of town. And somehow we rabbis don't understand the lack of attendance, and many of us judge them for it. (Understanding this foreign feeling, I have stopped with the judgment.)

But that's just my example as a rabbi. You can extend this to your workplace, your social peers, your family life — does everyone here know some secret set of rules or etiquette that you don't understand?

Maybe you're not lost, and you feel like you totally belong, but you are still beset by that most insipid of sensations: You are bored as hell. You are exactly where you think you belong, but you feel there's no more to learn or understand, and your mind is not challenged. You get all the jokes, but they are not funny. You sense there must be more to life, must be something deeper to understand about your surroundings, but how to go deeper or move beyond the mundane eludes you.

In my experience of being bored and of talking to bored people, boredom has two possible sources: 1) You are in a situation where you expect to be entertained, but your experience is not entertaining, or 2) you don't understand what's going on, so you can't appreciate those elements designed to engage you.

In the first case, it's not your fault that what you're doing is boring, but it is your responsibility to change what you're doing if you'd like to be more effectively entertained. Change the channel, walk out of the movie, put down the book, feign the need to go to the bathroom and exit the inane conversation. In the second case, it is also not your fault, and it is still your responsibility to disengage, or you can take on the heavier responsibility of gaining deeper understanding, especially if you know the boring activity is good for you.

Are you bored? (I hope not; I'm trying to keep this book as entertaining as possible.)

Seriously, do you find your life, or certain aspects of it, boring?

I do, too. But I usually find that the more I learn, the less bored I am, in general.

I've heard it said that if you don't want to be bored, don't be boring. The key to not be boring is to have something to say, and the key to have something to say is to learn something new. Or at least, new to you.

There are many aspects of life that seem to discourage curiosity. Author Seth Godin and others have observed that the modern education system itself was designed to produce obedient factory workers, not encourage intel-lectual curiosity. Even so-called knowledge work — data mining and information processing in the cube farms of the modern commercial economy — is essentially factory work, pumping out a known commodity while optimizing cost efficiency by following a clearly defined set of rules. This also discourages curiosity and creativity, unless you're curious about how to make the same old process even more efficient at cranking out the same old thing.

Where You Are Going

The good news is that all of these conditions — feeling lost, feeling foreign, feeling bored out of your gourd — are treatable, perhaps even curable. You can gain the insight to pick a worthy destination, and then find your right path (or at least your "right now" path) to get there. You can learn the language and the customs of the community where you already belong, or where you hope to belong. You can inoculate yourself to boredom (and *keep* from being boring) by better understanding the world so you can engage it at a deeper level.

How? By unwrapping the Gift of Learning. By select-ing a course of study to pursue and by making time for it every day, you will begin feeling less lost, and before long, totally at home. You will grow more familiar, comfortable, and confident in a world you begin to understand better. And you will feel less and less bored, not only because you will have greater understanding and appreciation for the world around you, but also because by learning regularly, you will become less and less . . . boring.

By making learning a daily part of your routine, you can broaden your perspective on the world and deepen your understanding of it. You begin to see the various paths that stretch out before you, including the one that you may already be on, and make an informed judgment about how to proceed. You begin to form a clear picture of where you'd like to go — set better goals — and thus be empowered to move in that direction. As Lewis Carroll illustrated in the conversation between Alice and the Cheshire Cat, if you don't know where you are going, any road can take you there; however, with a clearer destination in mind, as informed by your learning, you can be more selective and wise about the path you travel, pick the right road, and proceed with confidence. Will it always be easy? Absolutely not. But the right road, even with potholes, traffic jams, and detours, will get you where you're going much faster than traveling the wrong road unimpeded.

The cure for boredom isn't necessarily thrill-seeking adventure. In my experience adventure often just makes one more sensitive to boredom in non-thrilling environments. It's certainly not drugs or alcohol; they merely dull your standards for what's interesting (or attractive, or safe). The surest cure, I found, is constant learning — understanding the world around you better and better each day.

But learning isn't just about knowing more, it's about doing better. At every moment we are beset with the question: What's the next right action to take? What's the very best action to take under the circumstances, or is it wiser to do nothing and wait? So much frustration and boredom and feeling "stuck" comes from not knowing what action to take next, or not being able to decide among actions to take. Veiled in ignorance or indecision, we often do nothing, so nothing ever changes.

This is where the Gift of Learning can help. By devoting time to learning something new (or at least new to you) each day, you gradually become more and more interested in the world around you, and being more interested, you become more interesting to be around. Second, as you gain greater understanding of the observable (and unobservable) world and greater wisdom about how to act in the world, your actions become wiser, your decisions become better, and your moral compass becomes a more refined instrument.

There is an argument among rabbis in the Talmud about which is better: Learning or action (see the quote at the beginning of this chapter). Judaism, in general, concerns itself more with action than with thought, faith, or intention; all or nearly all of the commandments are interpreted to speak to visible action, not internal states, so naturally one of the rabbis (Rabbi Tarfon) says action is more important than study. Another rabbi disagrees and says study is more important because it leads to action. It seldom works the other way around.

What I call the Gift of Learning is the instruction of setting aside a regular time to study, so that your actions throughout the day become wiser and better, you understand the world around you better, and perhaps most important, you understand yourself better.

I'm putting this Gift first on the list because I believe it offers us the key habit that unlocks all the others. Fully unwrapping each of the other gifts requires a certain level of knowledge of how to get started; however, improving in each requires not only practice, but deeper understanding of the practice itself that comes from learning about it. And as you take on more and more of these practices with greater intensity and understanding, I promise that while you may feel frustrated at times, or you may feel like you don't know enough to progress, you won't be bored overall, and I hope you'll be inspired to learn ever more about each practice as a way to improve and reap greater benefits.

The Gift of Learning can make you not only more interested in the world around you; it can make you more interesting to others. It also fosters greater understanding of other cultures and ideas, which makes you more open-minded and empathetic, as well as greater understanding and depth of insight into your own culture and the ideas you already have, which makes you more self-aware and less prone to being fooled by things you either take for granted or take at face value.

What makes Jewish study different, in my opinion, from other religious inquiry is that it not only actively encourages debate — God smiles on God's children wrestling over the best way to do what's right — it also records all sides of the debate for posterity. The *Talmud*, a compendium of oral history of interpretation of the *Tanakh* (Hebrew Bible) and debate about its meaning from which we derive Jewish law and practice, is what distinguishes Judaism as it's practiced today from the Iron Age, animal-sacrificing religion of Hebrews in the time covered by the *Tanakh*. For any given question one might have about the Torah and other sacred literature, every possible take on it by rabbis of antiquity is recorded, and while the winner of a particular argument may be declared, and his position may have become normative to practice, the minority position is recorded in the text for posterity. This means all future generations can see all sides and reason for themselves whether they want to follow the norm or chart their own course. Debate is not only encouraged; it is canonized!

For every practice in this book (including Learning) there is a vast library of knowledge on how to best go about it, including a diversity of opinion and options. This means that you are never charting your path alone;

you have the wisdom of a hundred generations available to you, for only the price of sitting down to study. This doesn't mean that the path you chart is fully dictated for you. You will navigate the road in your own way; you just don't have to reinvent the wheel at each fork in the road.

Where It Comes From

There are stories in our sacred texts about a teacher named Rabbi Akiva, who lived around the years 50-135 CE (Common Era; see Glossary). But before he was Rabbi Akiva, he was just plain Akiva ben Yosef, an illiterate adult and a poor shepherd in the employ of Kalba Savu'a. Akiva was sweet on the boss's daughter, but she rebuffed him. "My father would never let me marry someone as poor as you, except maybe if he were a famous scholar and teacher of Torah." Dejected, he went about his shepherding business. How could an illiterate clod such as himself be a great scholar, when at the age of 40 he didn't know a single letter of the alphabet?

One day, when tending to his employer's flock, Akiva wandered into a cave in search of a lost lamb. He encountered an odd-looking rock formation: a flat stone with a hole in the middle, and above it a small stalactite dripping water, slowly but steadily, straight through the hole. Akiva surmised that the steady drops of water, over time, had worn the hole through the rock. He had an epiphany.

"If water, which is soft and weak, can penetrate the stone, which is hard," he reasoned, "surely the words of the Torah, which are strong and sure as iron, can penetrate the heart, which is merely soft flesh and blood."

At this moment, Akiva decided to start learning.

Legend has it that this 40-year-old shepherd then went to sit with the students in what was effectively

Kindergarten, to learn the Hebrew alphabet. "First he learned the difference between *alef* and *bet* (the first two letters of the Hebrew alphabet), then he went on to learn from *alef* to *taf* (from the first letter to the last)." From there he went on to learn the entire Torah, as well as the oral tradition of commentary and argument about its contents. As his reputation for learning grew, he began to attract students who wanted to learn from him. By the end of his life, when he was executed for teaching the Torah in defiance of the Roman Empire, he had attracted as many as 48,000 students.

And to think, at age 40, he didn't even know his ABCs.

This is the same Rabbi Akiva quoted in the beginning of this chapter: Learning is superior to action, because learning leads to correct action.

Where I Am

I was always a curious kid, and bright in some areas, but, as previously mentioned, I was easily bored. Even into adulthood, I found that once I had a sufficient grasp of an idea, the idea no longer interested me. Once I could see the bottom, I felt I had no reason to stay in the pool. As a kid in a part of the U.S. where evangelical Christianity rules the culture, I quickly came to the point in religious inquiry where my pastor, teacher, or a relative would say, "that's a mystery, and will need to remain a mystery — we don't ask questions about that." So I became bored with religious practice, including what I saw as its limited approach to learning, and it never quite stuck for me.

I studied finance and worked in financial analysis because I found the concepts and the math involved fascinating. But once I started working in the profession and found that most people didn't make decisions based on complicated concepts and hard math but by simple rules of thumb, corporate politics, and sales quotas, I could "see the bottom" of the field, and it no longer interested me. I used computer programming skills in my work, and I was always keen to learn a new coding language or programming method. But once I saw that most problems I was solving were relatively simple and straightforward, I felt once again like I could "see bottom" and grew bored.

In my mid-20s, when I started to dip my toe into studying the Torah, I discovered commentaries, and commentaries on commentaries *ad infinitum*, and read the sermons and articles of contemporary rabbis continuing to interpret this multi-layered tradition in new ways that shed wisdom on up-to-the-minute changes in the world. I quickly realized that the Torah, along with the wisdom and practices that have evolved from its study and practice through many cultures over thousands of years, is, in the words of my teacher Rabbi Joseph Schwartz, an infinite text of ultimately indeterminate meaning: There is no bottom. That's when I fell in love with a subject of study I would never be done with, never be bored with, and that's why, in the end, I have made learning the Torah (and teaching what I've learned) my life's work. While some of the day-to-day housekeeping of my job as a rabbi can be boring at times, when it comes to learning, I haven't been bored a single day since I started.

And to be clear: There's no book I've ever opened as a rabbi that you can't open, too.

What to Do

1. Set aside some time for daily learning.

Make a daily appointment for your brain with some good learning material. And I *mean* make an appointment:

Whatever you use for keeping track of your daily schedule — your smartphone, your desk calendar, a whiteboard on your fridge — block of time to learn and stick to it. I recommend starting in blocks of 30 minutes, if possible. You can do more if you like, but it should be something manageable you can stick to, at least until it becomes a habit. It can be any time of day — many believe learning in the evening just before sleep is best for memory retention — as long as it's the same time every day. As for content, I recommend starting with a good translation of the *Tanakh* ("Hebrew Bible" — see glossary). Even if you don't consider yourself a "Bible person" this can be helpful. First, you'll be surprised to discover all the stories and quotes and ideas expressed in modern culture that have biblical origins; your cultural literacy quotient will go way up! Second, you'll be forearmed for conversation with people who misquote and misuse the Bible to support bad ideas and bad behavior. Nevertheless, if you're timid about opening a religious text at first, any subject or material that can hold your attention for 30 minutes a day for the near future will suffice, as long as you feel like you're learning something. (NOTE: If you're totally a Bible person, and you prefer an edition with the New Testament attached, be my guest; I recommend getting the *Tanakh* anyway, because you might be surprised by some differences in the translations of certain stories when they are not considered a preamble to the New Testament.)

2. Take an Introduction to Judaism class, or similar.

A good Introduction to Judaism class will broaden your mind and deepen your understanding about all the Gifts covered in this book and many, many more. These classes are usually designed to give sufficient knowledge and understanding to someone who intends to convert to

Judaism; however, you never need to have that intention in order to take the class. (I didn't, when I took it.) It will give you historical context, as well as great examples of how all the Gifts in this book are implemented by diverse communities around the world today. I personally recommend (and teach) the Miller Introduction to Judaism program, which is based in Los Angeles but has affiliate programs all over the United States and is expanding its program globally, with new translations of the complete textbook and curriculum in Spanish. It is the best program of its kind I've seen, and I've seen quite a few. Taking this class will also connect you with other people who are on a similar journey to yours, and who couldn't use friends on a journey like this?

If at all possible, I encourage you to take a class like this in person, taught by a local rabbi. These are usually taught in synagogues, at times which are convenient for busy adults. First, contact the Miller program (http://intro.aju.edu) to see if a synagogue near you teaches their course. If not, contact synagogues in your area and find out whether they offer an Introduction to Judaism class. As a last resort, search online for virtual classes. I'm a huge fan of online learning and a firm believer in its potential impact; however, I believe this material benefits from personal presence and interaction. If this is not practical for you, by all means take an online class, but before you enroll, spend some time researching the reputation of the online course. Unlike humans, they are not all created equal.

3. Find yourself a teacher.

While it's possible to learn a lot on your own, you'll make faster and more focused progress on your journey if you have an experienced guide. You wouldn't try to summit Mount Everest without a *sherpa*, would you? (Not that there's any risk of hypothermia or oxygen deprivation where we're going.) The chief benefit of having a teacher or mentor in your chosen field of study is the combination of experience and relationship: A guide not only knows the terrain of where you're going, but also has the chance to get to know you personally, and thus can guide you toward the most helpful material for you to learn right now, and what to learn next, based on your unique goals, needs, and experience. If you're studying the Tanakh or other Jewish material recommended in this book, I recommend you connect with a local rabbi (tell her or him I sent you), explain your learning goals, and ask if they would be willing to meet with you occasionally to discuss what you're learning and what other resources you should consider. Most rabbis I know would be excited to talk to you about this, but if you find one who is not, ask another, and feel free to reach out to me if you need a referral — I have connections with rabbis all over the world who would be delighted to be your guide on this journey.

4. Find a study buddy.

Most journeys in life are improved by having a traveling companion, and the traditional practice of the Gift of Learning is no different. The rabbis of our tradition figured out a long time ago that the best way to learn is to approach your learning not only with a teacher who knows you, but also a friend who is more or less your equal in the learning at hand. I talk more about why this is so effective at the end of this book; for now, it's enough to find someone and get started together. One way to secure your study buddy is to share this book with a friend you think might be interested in it or helped by it, and asking them to read it and take the recommended steps with you. If you can't think of anyone, or feel weird asking, talk to your teacher and see if they have other students at your level with whom you could partner up. Agree on a regular time and place to meet, agree on the material you'll be learning together (you should be looking at the same text), and then get together and discuss what you've been learning on your own. You will be amazed how another person's read of the same material will open your mind to new interpretations, and each of you will be grateful to have someone to help you when you get stuck on something.

5. Join a learning community.

As you get deeper into the learning you're doing with your teacher and your study buddy, you will benefit greatly from getting involved in a community of people on a similar journey. You will be informed and inspired by those who are a little farther along than you are, and perhaps in surprising ways, you will be gratified by that moment when you discover that you are an inspiration (and perhaps a teacher yourself) to those who are following in your footsteps. Later in this book we'll focus in greater detail on the Gift of Community. For now, it's enough that you seek out a group of people engaged in the same work of this Gift of Learning. This can be a synagogue or other religious institution that hosts one or more classes. This community can even be found by taking a single class, like the Introduction class I recommended earlier. It could just as easily be found in taking an extension class on car repair or a regular class at a yoga studio. What's most important is that you form social connections among those with whom you have an intellectual connection and shared curiosity. This social connection reinforces that you are on the right track, and over time you will join or form a whole group of people to inspire and support you, whom you will in turn support and inspire.

THE SECOND GIFT
GRATITUDE

"Who is rich? One who rejoices in his portion."
— *Pirkei Avot* 4:1

"If you've forgotten the language of gratitude,
you'll never be on speaking terms with happiness."
— C. Neil Strait

Building a daily habit of counting blessings and expressing gratitude helps you internalize all the meaning and joy you already have in your life. This practice fosters an "attitude of gratitude" and a disposition of abundance as an antidote to the feeling of being or having less than you should.

Where You Are

One of the most powerful forces in our lives — a force for positive change, as well as a force for destruction and depression — is dissatisfaction. The sense of not having enough or not being enough can be motivating, debilitating, or both.

Dissatisfaction has driven people to invent new solutions to common problems and build billion-dollar businesses. Dissatisfaction with one's career has sent people back to school to train for a new one (like that one time I left a lucrative consulting career and went to seminary for five years). Dissatisfaction with poor health leads people to transform their habits and transform their bodies. Dissatisfaction with the life of being an addict has motivated people to join support groups to kick alcohol, drugs, cigarettes, gambling, unhealthy sex — you name it. Dissatisfaction with the status quo has been at the root of every major innovation in history and has changed and improved untold millions, if not billions, of lives.

But dissatisfaction in another sense — the sense of not being enough or not having enough — can also ruin a life. It can lead to overwork, gluttony, or even a paralyzing shame-spiral of inaction. Just as sure as dissatisfaction can break us of addiction, it can also break us *with* addiction — pursuing the path of continuing to feed the dragon (as my friends in addiction recovery work say), hoping that the next drink, hit, or hand of cards will be *enough*. Spoiler alert: It never is, and it never will be.

Where You Are Going

The secret about satisfaction and dissatisfaction lies in choosing among the itches that are good to scratch and those that aren't, choosing when to keep going with work or consumption and when, instead, to say, "That's enough, thank you very much."

Sometimes it's valuable to say "thank you, that's enough," even as we keep going.

This next Gift — the Gift of Gratitude — is about recognizing and acknowledging those aspects of our lives where we can be satisfied and grateful for what we have, as well as understand and appreciate when what we do have comes from outside of ourselves, so we can mitigate the ingratitude, the craving, the feeling of lack and un-wholeness that leads to depression and the destructive kind of ambition. Only when we are truly grateful for what we already have, I believe, can we healthfully ask and expect more from others, and more from ourselves . . . even more from God.

The Gift of Gratitude is couched primarily in the vocabulary and syntax of blessing: We regularly bless God, or describe God as blessed, in a hundred different ways, acknowledging that, for all our own ingenuity and hard work, God is the ultimate source of our all our blessings. Though some work tirelessly to perfect their bodies, we didn't create our own bodies. Though some exercise great force and creativity in shaping the world around them, no single one of us created the world as our canvas for improvement. Whether or not you believe that God created the universe and created us to work and play in it, you can still acknowledge that *you* created neither the universe, nor humanity, nor even your nascent self. You have to admit that these things were given to you, to do with what you will, and it's healthy to acknowledge this every once in a while with gratitude and humility.

Traditionally, Jews make it a practice to say a hundred blessings every day. In many communities this begins each day with an individual waking up and acknowledging that the Author of All Blessings allowed us to wake to another day and try again. We then bless God for all the ways in which God made us unique, powerful, and capable. People attend prayer services in which God's gifts to humanity are acknowledged, even as we petition for ongoing help and support, and we continue to pray for the seemingly impossible, namely: Peace and wholeness in a world that seems to keep breaking down despite our best efforts. We bless God as the source of our sustenance before each meal, and we often end meals with further blessings of gratitude for the bread which gives us the strength to fulfill both our own desires and our larger purpose. Finally, we go to bed blessing God as protector and sustainer, entrusting God with our soul and consciousness, trusting that it will be restored to us when we wake to another day, another chance.

If this sounds like a lot to remember, a lot to do throughout the beginning, middle, and end of a long, busy day, you're not wrong. It is a lot. And remembering and doing all of it is a spiritual discipline built up over time, with practice, little by little. But the more you pause for gratitude over gifts in your life both mundane and magnificent, the more you move through the world with a sense of wholeness and peace, better able to focus on those tasks and aspiration where *you* are the source of blessing for your own life and for others.

See, we're not in charge of everything. We're not responsible for everything in our own lives, good or bad. But we spend an inordinate amount of time worrying about things that are beyond our control, and desiring things that are beyond our need or capacity to really enjoy. And we then blame all of that wasted time and energy for not getting to our most important work, for not being able to focus on that which merits our unique skill, insight, and application.

What if you honestly felt like you *possess* enough, and that everything you add to your life is just a blessed bonus?

What if you honestly felt like you *are* enough, and that every way in which you continue to grow is not a slow grinding step toward sufficiency, but a great leap forward from one place of strength, to another place of greater strength?

This is the promise of the "attitude of gratitude" you can cultivate from unwrapping this Gift.

Where It Comes From

There's a powerful passage that jumps off the page at me every time I read it, mostly because it's such a real distillation of human nature. It comes from the Book of Deuteronomy, most of which is Moses' final speech to the people he's led across the wilderness for their entire lives, instructing them how to behave once they enter the Promised Land, a place where he cannot follow to continue guiding them. In this passage, he warns them to not let their future prosperity cause them to forget where they came from, and Who helped them along the way:

> "When you have eaten your fill, and have built fine houses to live in, and your herds and flocks have multiplied, and your silver and gold have increased, and everything you own has prospered, beware lest your heart grow haughty and you forget the Lord your God — who freed you from the land of Egypt, the house of bondage; who led you through the great and terrible wilderness with its serpents and scorpions, a parched land with no water in it, who brought forth water for you from the flinty rock; who fed you in the wilderness with manna, which your fathers had never known, in order to test you by hardships only to benefit you

in the end — and you say to yourselves, "My own power and the might of my own hand have won this wealth for me." Remember that it is the Lord your God who gives you the power to get wealth, in fulfillment of the covenant that God made on oath with your ancestors, as is still the case. If you do forget the Lord your God and follow other gods to serve them or bow down to them, I warn you this day that you shall certainly perish."

(Deuteronomy 8:12-19)

Now, whether you're a Bible person, or a God person, or not, you have to admit that the author (or Author) of this text has our number: It is the nature of humanity that we all have the potential to become to be a bunch of ungrateful and self-centered children. Our tendency is to take all the credit for everything we have and everything we've accomplished, when in reality, we have nothing, and we accomplish nothing without the help of others, whether we actively cooperated with them or even know who they were.

To borrow an example from my teacher, Rabbi Bradley Shavit Artson, I wear a shirt every single day. Except maybe on vacation, if it's super-hot outside. That said, I have never in my life *made* a shirt. Except for that one time, at age 6, for my teddy bear, and it was a pathetic shirt. The bear looked sad. Suffice it to say, I get to wear clothes every day regardless of my inability to make clothes worth wearing. I love to cook, but I venture to say that I would make a terrible farmer, so the food I cook is all enabled by the labor and ingenuity of someone else, just like the clothes I wear. And even for those who make the clothes, as rough as that job might be, their livelihood depends on the person who figured out how to process the cotton plant into cloth. And who invented cotton in the first place?

We're back to the God question again, but in any case, my point is this: Everything you have and everything you accomplish, regardless of what you put into it, depends on someone or something else, and that source (or Source) deserves a little gratitude. And beyond the gratitude that is deserved and the credit that is due, think about this: What does it do for you to express that gratitude, to develop the gratitude habit, to become a more grateful person in general?

Expressing gratitude — and more: becoming habitually accustomed to expressing gratitude — reminds us that all our success and even our sustenance are interconnected with the labor, success, sustenance, and care of others. Our very existence — the fact that we wake up in the morning — is contingent.

Realizing this may be troubling at first. Being so dependent on others (and even, as some believe, being dependent on God), are we ultimately powerless to shape our own destiny?

Not in my book. We absolutely have the power to shape our destiny, even if it is constantly co-created by others. Being depending on others doesn't mean you are helpless. Quite the contrary: It means you are helped.

Where I Am

I remember the very moment when I stopped believing in God.

I also remember the very moment when I started again.

First things first: I stopped believing in God the moment I read about halfway through a certain book — I forget the page, but who knows whether the edition is still in print — when I was probably 17 or 18 years old. I'd borrowed a copy of Mikhael Bulgakov's *The Master and Margarita* from my elder sister, and in that book, it gives a plausible (to teenage me, anyway) alternative to a common religious narrative, and at that moment, prepared as I was by a rationalist tendency and natural teenage skepticism, all the religious training and well-constructed belief fell like a house of cards. I was an arrogant kid, a smug intellectual beyond his years, and I thought I was too smart to believe in God.

Even at the moment I became Jewish, I didn't believe. I was curious about the people and its traditions, I was motivated as a father of Jewish children to be the best and most knowledgeable father I could be, and I decided to take an Introduction to Judaism class. During that class, I fell in love with Judaism — the people, the traditions, the intellectual rigor, and even the religious practice — but I still couldn't believe, in the sense that I felt compelled by the Christian community to believe in something specific to belong. It was only when I discovered the existence of proud Jewish atheists — as proud of their Jewishness as they were certain of the non-existence of God — that I felt comfortable take the steps toward become Jewish myself.

But a little while later, something changed. There was one evening, when I was in my late 20s, that I looked back on my life, and I marveled. I remember thinking about that very word: Marvel. (Not just because of my childhood affinity for comic books.) And what's surprising to think about today is that I marveled not at what good things I had accomplished at that point in my life, but what bad things I had avoided.

See, I was a wild kid. I've always been a risk-taker. In my early years, that meant trying to get myself lost on purpose while traveling with my family in foreign countries. Later, in my teenage years, that meant experimenting with alcohol, drugs, and other high-risk, less-than-healthy, less-than-legal shenanigans. Luckily, it also meant taking a risk and getting married at age 19, later graduating from college with a wife and two children. Because if I hadn't taken that risk, along with cleaning up my act as a father, I would have followed my friends who were getting into harder drugs and more dangerous behavior. All my close friends survived those experiences long enough to mend their ways, but there's no guarantee that I would have.

And despite starting adulthood behind the 8-Ball (if you'll forgive the pun), I was fine. Despite making choices that could have seriously impaired my physical and mental health, put me in jail, hurt other people, or even ended my life, I was fine. Was I perfectly happy? No. Had I accomplished everything I'd wanted to accomplish by that age? Not yet. Was I blessed, truly blessed, to get to wake up every morning and try again? In that moment, I realized I was. I was blessed to draw breath, despite making a hundred decisions in my past that could have taken that blessing away. I was blessed that my parents met, blessed that they got married, blessed that they had me, without any input or assistance on my part. I was blessed to have two healthy sons at that time. I was blessed that people took a chance on me — my teachers, my wife, my employers — when they just as easily could have invested their time, energy, and love in someone else. I had my heartaches and disappointments and pain, just like everyone did and does, and I did work my tail off for many of the accomplishments and successes I had achieved by that point, but in that moment, I realized that I also had advantages and kindnesses and just plain dumb luck showered upon me without my doing anything, certainly beyond what I could say I *deserved*.

And in that moment, I started to believe that there must be at least some sort of active love in the universe that takes care of people, and perhaps more importantly, takes an active interest in how people take care of each other. That was the moment that my heart opened back up to the idea or the feeling that I'm talking about when I talk about God.

That was also the moment that I was overwhelmed by gratitude. I had worked a lot and achieved a little, to be sure, but I also had things and people and experiences and lessons and grace in my life that was far beyond anything that I could have accomplished on my own. That's when I started saying "thank you" more often, whether to people who helped me out in the world or people close to me whom I took for granted. That's the moment I started, well, I guess you could call it praying, on a somewhat regular basis. Sure, I'd prayed in those foxhole moments; even when I thought I didn't believe, there's no *not* praying in that hospital room when your first child is being born, praying for everything to turn out OK. That's not praying, really, not how I did it; it's begging. But after that moment of clarity about all that was going right in my life in ways I wasn't entitled to, the ratio of begging to thanking in my prayers flipped.

I still beg from time to time — usually when the physical and mental well-being of those I care about is on the line — but I thank a lot more, and when I do, I feel better in general about my life than when I don't acknowledge my blessings on the regular. I have no illusion that either this book or my work as a rabbi is going to make me rich. That's OK. Because I already possess the wealth of rejoicing in what I already have, and the habit of articulating gratitude reminds me of that wealth every day.

What to Do

1. Practice waking in gratitude.

Try saying "thank you," in some way, at the moment you wake up every morning. This can be directed at God, at the universe, at the rising sun, at the person you wake up next to, if you're so blessed, or even to your own beating heart, for not stopping while you slept. There is a traditional Jewish practice of saying a prayer every morning when we wake up: "I am grateful to you, living and enduring Sovereign, that you have restored my soul to me in compassion, so great is your faithfulness." Some ancient peoples thought their souls departed at night while they slept, and the fact that it returns each day, along with our consciousness, is a sign of God's trustworthiness. More simply put, we wake up thanking God for compassionately allowing us to wake up! Wherever you choose to direct your gratitude, practicing the act of starting each day with words of thanks is a small but powerful way to orient yourself toward approaching each day with gratitude pre-programmed. Sometimes you'll forget, and maybe remember to say it later, and that's OK. It's about practice, not perfection.

2. Practice gratitude for health.

Every morning (maybe while you're brushing your teeth) look in the mirror and marvel how well put-together you are. Spend 30 seconds acknowledging all the things about you that totally work without your conscious effort, before you go looking for flaws and things to improve. Try not to giggle: There's also a traditional Jewish prayer we're supposed to say every time we go to the bathroom. I know, right? It may seem picayune, and to some even perverse, but the content of the prayer is essentially this: Blessed are you, God, who has fashioned such an intricate piece of machinery as the human body! If any of its many small, moving pieces were to malfunction — an opening to close up, or something to open when it shouldn't — we couldn't survive. This prayer is acknowledging that every human being, upon completing its most mundane, animal activity, has reason to be profoundly grateful, because . . . oh, man, imagine the alternative! You might ask: What if my health doesn't inspire gratitude? Then perhaps you can express gratitude for what does work, because that sustains you to face what doesn't. We can thank Heaven for small miracles, even when we don't get the big ones, but all the more so when we do.

3. Express gratitude before and after sustenance.

Try this: Next time you eat or drink something, say "thank you" or offer your blessing to its source before taking the first bite or the first sip. You may do the working, the earning, the shopping, and the cooking for everything you consume; you may do one part of that process, or none of it. Nevertheless, it's valuable to consider and acknowledge that you didn't invent food, that many forces, seen and unseen, come together with the express purpose to nourish you, to take care of your needs. In that moment of recognition, how cared for do you feel? Then, when you're done eating, take a moment and say another "thank you" or blessing for being satisfied. While many faith traditions practice saying Grace before a meal, Judaism book-ends this by asking us to recite a series of blessings after a meal any time three or more people break bread together.

4. Take the Thank-You Note Challenge.

Ready to be challenged? Resolve that for 30 days, you will send at least one note of thanks to one person in your life every day for something they've done for you. You can set yourself up for success before this challenge by buying a stack of 30 thank-you cards (and 30 stamps — no excuses!), or by setting a daily reminder on your smartphone (better, a 15-minute daily appointment in your calendar app) to send a quick email to someone who did something nice for you, gave you something you wanted or needed, or helped you out in some way. Observe how you feel and how other people react to your gratitude after the 30 days.

5. Join a gratitude community.

Experiment with daily prayer services or daily yoga practice at synagogue, church, or studio near you. In most faith traditions, as well as in most yoga classes I've experienced, there is a significant amount of time allocated to the public expression of gratitude to the Source of our blessings. This usually involves enumerating aloud or meditating on our blessings and the miracles in our lives, both great and small, which can be moving when we catch ourselves feeling lucky for what we have, regardless of what we want. Doing this in a community with other people is great for socially reinforcing the Gift of Gratitude and fostering a shared sense of abundance, especially when we do it early in the morning, inoculating us with Gratitude before we face a world that seems to push us toward competition, scarcity, and want. If you tried the first action of practicing waking in gratitude, and we agree how powerful it is for you to reprogram your mind away from waking in dread of the selfish rat race, toward instead starting the day with gratitude for all the races you've already won, how powerful would it be to start the day celebrating with others all the races we've already won together, and to be there for others to help them celebrate?

THE THIRD GIFT
DISTINCTION

"Three types of people go down to Hell and do not return: one who sleeps with another man's wife, one who humiliates his friend in public, and one who spreads a bad name about his friend. But isn't humiliation and a bad name the same thing? No. The latter applies even if his friend isn't humiliated, because he is accustomed to the bad name."

— *Bava Metzia* 58b

"The word 'discipline' often evokes strong emotional reactions, particularly because it is often used synonymously with 'punishment.' However, the original meaning of discipline is 'to teach.'"

— Shauna L. Shapiro

There's more to being "kosher" than checking the ingredients of what we eat. Unwrapping the Gift of Distinction, that is, exercising mindfulness and

discipline in the quality of what we share with others —
in how we speak to and about others, in how and with
whom we conduct our intimate relationships — is just
as important as being careful about what we take in
through our diet. This Gift helps you "edit" your life
and refine it into a work of art.

Where You Are

Have you ever eaten something you later regretted
eating? Perhaps it made you feel sick, or guilty. Maybe
there are certain foods that hit the Achilles heel of your
self-control: You can't only eat just one. And half-way
through eating it, or maybe looking back at the empty
bag, tummy aches aside, beyond feeling like you lost
control over your eating, you had a depressing sensation
of losing control in general, of being out of control of
your life.

It's OK. We've all done it.

Have you ever been hurt by gossip? By someone else
spreading a rumor about something you did or said,
whether you did it or said it or not? Alternatively, have
you been hurt by something someone said to your face,
something overly critical or mean spirited? Perhaps
someone hurt you by reminding you, or reminding
others in your presence, about a bad habit of yours
you're working hard to overcome . . . or have overcome
successfully! What's the use of making a change in your
life if people still remember — and remind you — of
how bad you used to be?

I've been there. This is common, and just because
it's painful doesn't mean people don't do it all the time.

Have you ever felt used? You know: That feeling
when someone interacted with you in a way you thought
was out of shared interest, or appreciation, or love, that

turned out to be a manipulation to satisfy their own interests, goals, or pleasure. You were a means to their end, rather than an end unto yourself, this whole time.

Yeah . . . me, too. And the only thing worse than that feeling is the knowledge that it happens all the time, to people all around the world.

Sorry to dig all this stuff up. My intention was not to hurt you by reminding you of your weakness or the weakness of others. Rather, I wanted to point out that the suffering you've experienced by what you've taken in, or the guilt and regret you've experienced by what you've put out into the world, is not merely common: It's universal. And I'd like to suggest to you that the way out of feeling this pain in the future is not to fight it, but to rise above it, to set yourself apart, to distinguish yourself by acting in ways that distinguish you from those still mired in the consumption and production of pain.

Would you like to know how?

Where You Are Going

This chapter is in many ways the hardest for me to write because even though my core belief is that Jewish practices for growth are available and effective for everyone, everywhere, at some point, to make meaningful change in your life, you have to separate yourself from others. Though I believe our lives flourish in proportion to the quantity and quality of our connections with other people, to achieve quality, we sometimes must edit our quantity. Sometimes the best way to reduce the pain we feel is not to confront and defeat the source of that pain, but to disengage and rise above it, to separate and distinguish ourselves from others, or at least from the behavior we once had in common.

This is hard. In our core, I think many of us still hold on to that inner teenager: We want to be special, just like everyone else. We want to be recognized for our uniqueness, feel seen and valued for our unique characteristics and contributions to the world, but at the same time, we so long to fit in that few of us embrace the risk, the uncertainty of choosing to be different. The cost of separating ourselves from the herd is that it's lonely out there on the plain, and that's where the coyotes get you. It takes real maturity, real bravery, and the kind of audacity for which we're afraid others might judge us, to rise above the destructive habits and relationships that feel so natural that they give us comfort, even though they cause us pain.

The Gift of Distinction is a combination of Jewish disciplines that all have the same feature: They require us to make difficult decisions about everyday habits that often mark us for belonging to a larger group. You don't necessarily have to leave the groups or relationships you are in, but to reap the benefit of this Gift requires changing how we interact with others in a way that may feel antisocial at first. Unwrapping this Gift requires exercising Distinction in what we take in and what we put out, what we tolerate for ourselves and what we tolerate from others, in three fundamental dimensions of human existence and interaction: diet, communication, and relationships.

Diet

You're probably familiar with the word "kosher," most often used to describe a hot dog at a ball park, a dill pickle in the grocery aisle, or a special kind of meal on an airplane. (Remember meals on airplanes? Fondly? Amiright?) You may have also heard the word to describe whether a business deal was above-board or not: "Something about this contract just isn't kosher." You may even be familiar with kosher restaurants in your area where you can't get cheese on your burger or pepperoni on your pizza. You can thank Exodus 23:19 for that one, which says: "You shall not cook a kid in its mother's milk."

The work kosher comes from the Hebrew word *kasher* which means "fit" or "appropriate." In modern usage it most often describes food; something is kosher if it is sourced and prepared in ways consistent with the dietary laws laid out in the Torah (and later elaborated in the Talmud and Jewish legal codes), and is thus fit or appropriate for someone who follows those laws to eat. *Kashrut* (the laws and practices outlining appropriate behavior) is bigger than what's on the menu, however; it can also describe what is appropriate in other realms of human interaction such as speech, relationships, business dealings, and other areas of human interaction or ritual activity. For the purposes of this book, I use the word Distinction instead of *kashrut*.

First, I don't want you to think you have to be a Hebrew scholar to achieve real growth (the Gift of Learning notwithstanding). Second, I see the same principles of fit and appropriate behavior applying to multiple areas of life, and I don't want you to think the Gift of Distinction is just about food. The same language we use for food can be used for how we communicate and how we behave toward those we love.

Nevertheless, food is important! Not only is it the fuel of our very existence — every living thing takes in nutrients from an external source to live — it is also a source of personal pleasure and integral to our social interactions as well. We all eat to live, and some of us live to eat. (This guy.) Most people in the world get to eat every day, and in wealthier parts of the world, some people eat ritually three times a day or more, and some people eat, ahem, improvisationally between those times. It is perhaps the most basic human activity, besides reproduction, which we share with all living things. In fact, many humans never reproduce, but we all eat, some of us much more than others. (This guy.)

It is that which is most common that we often take most for granted. Because eating is so common, exercising mindfulness and, if you like, spiritual discipline, around something that you may do several times a day, something that is essential for your very survival and well-being, can accomplish a powerful elevation of that which we so often take for granted and relegate to a mundane and unremarkable activity, to our great loss. I therefore recommend you consider enhancing your eating habits by setting some boundaries.

I describe the nature and source of source of these boundaries in greater detail later on, but here is the essence: For the most part, Jewish dietary laws and traditions concern themselves with whether and how we eat animals. To eat the flesh of another being means taking its life. (This is an assumption, of course: not to be too graphic, but one of the first dietary rules in the Torah is not to eat part or all of a creature which is still alive.) Given that by eating meat, we are taking a life to fortify and support our own, it is incumbent upon us to treat that life with some measure of respect, and much of the dietary laws concern the proper way to harvest animals so that their suffering is minimized. Further, the Torah puts certain animals off-limits altogether, not because they were considered sacred, but because people viewed them as unfit or unworthy for human consumption. Finally, we have a restriction on separating meat-based foods from dairy foods, to strictly observe the tenet stated earlier (and repeated twice more in the Torah) not to cook a kid in its own mother's milk. Our people recognized a long time ago that slaughtering an animal only to cook it in that substance which was intended to give it life represented the lowest and most perverse form of animal cruelty.

You might notice that most of the fuss here is about eating meat, and if you think that a vegetarian or vegan diet avoids a lot of this fuss, you're right. Many Jews, like many people worldwide, observe a strict vegetarian diet for spiritual as well as health reasons, and it is noted by the sages of our tradition that in the biblical account of the Garden of Eden, not only were the people instructed to eat only fruits and grains; even the lions and tigers were vegetarian! The first time we observe people eating meat is after the famous flood, and Noah doesn't come on the scene until 10 generations after Adam and Eve.

Communication

There's more to editing our behavior, however, than being mindful of what we take in. It's also important to be conscious that what we put out into the world — that is, how we communicate and otherwise relate to our fellow humans — is fit for human consumption.

In the Jewish tradition, there is a long-held value of avoiding what is called *lashon hara* (Hebrew: "wicked tongue" or "evil speech"). While in reality, Jews tend to gossip just as much as any other people, many practice the discipline of avoiding talking about other people at all when they are not around. This is not limited to spreading negative falsehoods; we avoid talking about another's negative qualities or situation even if saying it would be true. In this case, we avoid spreading a bad name about someone who might otherwise have fine qualities, or be actively be working to reform their bad habits.

We also avoid sharing even kind information about others. Why? Try to imagine a conversation in which you tell someone something nice about a third party: "Karen is a great cook!" Once you've opened the door to the conversation about someone else, the person you are talking to may be tempted to share something less kind: "But her brisket once gave me heartburn," or, "Yes, but her kitchen is a mess," or, "I only wish her son was such a good cook, too."

You can imagine this practice of avoiding *lashon hara* could create a difficulty around something like being a professional reference for another person. How can you serve as a reference for someone, even a good one, if you can't talk about them? The solution: You can speak about yourself: i.e. "I'd hire him again," or, "If I had an opening like you have, I'd hire her for it." If your reference is not a good one, it is permissible to share limited information, but only that which is relevant to the job being filled, if you believe doing so will prevent the employer from being harmed, physically or economically: i.e. "Handling fragile glassware in the role you describe does not play to Karen's strengths," but you can't say, "And she also has poor taste in sweaters." While this may be true, it is not relevant to the position, unless she would be handling glassware for a sweater boutique (?!). Of course, it is permitted to report someone to the authorities if you believe someone intends to harm another person or their property.

Whereas the practice of avoiding *lashon hara* pertains to how you communicate *about* someone, we have another ancient tradition of Distinction in how you speak *to* someone. We are not permitted to speak to someone in a way that might either embarrass them (once more, even if the content of the communication is true) or mislead them in a way that might bring them to harm or loss. This kind of talk is called *ona'at devarim*, or oppressive speech. This includes calling someone by an embarrassing nickname, even if they are used to it, or reminding someone of their past bad behavior once they've made amends and reformed themselves, for example: "Hey, Stinky, old man, I'm really impressed how you've turned things around, but remember when we used to go out and steal cars together?"

It also includes misleading people in business. The example given in the sources: "Don't tell a donkey driver that so-and-so might have a load of grain for him to transport, if you know this not to be true." See, the donkey driver was like the long-haul trucker of his day, and if he came to you looking to haul something, and you gave him a false lead to get him out of your face, you were not only misleading him for your own gain; you were also wasting his time by sending him on a wild grain chase. Some say you shouldn't ask a shopkeeper how much an item costs if you have no intention of buying it; the shopkeeper might get his hopes up falsely about making a sale. One might say the modern equivalent of this is walking into a Best Buy store to check out the picture quality on a new TV, when you fully intend to get the same model TV for less from Amazon.com. Of course, you are permitted to check out the TV in person if you legitimately intend to buy it there if they have the best price, and then buy it somewhere else if you discover they have a better price. The point is, this Gift of Distinction forbids misleading people about your intentions in ways that might bring them to embarrassment, harm, or even wasted time they could use to help other customers whose intentions are more sincere.

Most telling of our sages' opinion of the seriousness of embarrassing someone is their likening it to physical harm:

> "A sage taught in the presence of Rav Naḥman bar Yitzḥak: Anyone who humiliates another in public, it is as though he were spilling blood. Rav Naḥman bar Yitzḥak said to him: You have spoken well, as we see that after the humiliated person blushes, the red leaves his face and pallor comes in its place, which is tantamount to spilling his blood."
>
> (*Bava Metzia* 58b)

Look, no one is perfect in how we talk to and about people, but I think taking someone's feelings and reputation as seriously as you take their right to live unharmed is a powerful aspiration that you might find cleansing, elevating for you personally, and at the same time doing your small part to cleanse your corner of the world of this kind of negativity and harm. Certainly, if everyone practiced this, Twitter would collapse tomorrow (or else it might become a powerful medium for lifting people up); however, just because we can't expect everyone to aspire to this level of Distinction and kindness in the world, that doesn't mean each of us doesn't get to try. Each of us has the power to improve in this area, and all of us reap the benefits when one of us succeeds.

In a nutshell, just as there is Distinction to be observed that what we take into our bodies is appropriate and fitting for our spiritual well-being, so too may we benefit from practicing Distinction that what we put into the world via communication to and about people is fitting and appropriate for the kind of world we want to live in, a world that thrives on honesty and empathy rather than on humiliation and deception.

Relationships

There is one more aspect to the Gift of Distinction I want to share with you, and that is exercising care in personal relationships. This not only includes intimate, romantic relationships; some of the same principles extend to close friendships, casual acquaintances, people at the office, and even the guy at the post office.

To start with those very closest relationships — those which involve sexual intimacy — while the Jewish tradition has evolved, and while different denominations have different party lines on things like homosexuality and premarital sex, what's consistent throughout time and across communities is that sexual intimacy should never be coercive or degrading. To be clear, Judaism is quite sex-positive. We view sex between committed partners to be just as essential to cementing bonds of intimacy and friendship as it is essential for procreation, and whatever two consenting adults wish to do to enjoy one another's company is OK in our book, as long as neither party is being forced against their will or put in a position they find degrading. The Gift of Distinction in intimate relationships means mutual consent and mutual respect. If those criteria are satisfied . . . Game on.

But beyond sexual relationships, that mutual consent and respect speaks to the larger value behind all relationships: Mutual appreciation for the integrity and inherent dignity of the other. The Jewish philosopher Martin Buber wrote a book in the early 20ᵗʰ Century called *I and Thou* in which he describes this mutual appreciation as a spectrum between two poles: "I-Thou" relationships and "I-It" relationships.

"I-Thou" refers to relating to someone with full appreciation for their independent existence as a human being, with their own hopes, dreams, plans, and intrinsic worth, regardless of their interaction or interdependence with you. This requires fully seeing the person as an end unto themselves, rather than as a means to your end. This describes, for example, a healthy relationship between spouses or close friends, each with their own worth and own goals independent of their interaction with each other, in addition to any shared goals of the partnership.

In an "I-It" relationship, by contrast, you relate to another human being only insofar as they are a means to your end. For example, let's say you live in a big city and go to a large bank in which you wait in a single long line and are randomly assigned to a teller based on who's free at the moment. It's unlikely you know the teller you are working with, and your perception of his value to you is limited to the efficiency with which he handles your transaction, presumably one that could not be handled easily by a drive-up machine outside the bank. Your relationship to the teller in the moment of your transaction is likely an "I-It" relationship; the teller is instrumental to meeting your needs, but the transaction neither requires nor encourages you to consider the teller's intrinsic worth as a person, with his own hopes, dreams, etc.

Don't feel bad. You, too, are instrumental to the teller, not as a human being of infinite intrinsic worth and with an urgent need to change a bill for a roll of quarters for the laundry machine to wash your lucky shirt for an interview at a greeting card company, where you will hopefully fulfill your dream of monetizing your master's degree in poetry, finally making your parents proud, validating your life choices, and proving your third-grade teacher wrong about your literary promise. No such ends of yours matter to the teller, only that you're another customer that keeps the bank open and his job secure. You have an "I-It" relationship with each other, and that's fine as far as it goes. Sometimes you just need a roll of quarters.

But Buber suggests that when you truly relate to someone on an "I-Thou" level, you catch a glimpse of the Divine: As each one of us is created in the image of God, each of us is intrinsically worthy of the dignity and respect due to the Holy One, regardless of what they can or cannot do for you in the moment. Buber believes that seeing the divinity of our Source in each other enables the highest form of respect, service, and love in a relationship. Like I said, sometimes you just need a roll of quarters, or a stamp at the post office, or a pizza delivered, or a driver's license renewed, and the name and the story of the person delivering that service is irrelevant to its delivery *per se*. But how much better might we walk in the world if we let ourselves care about the story of the pizza man? We might be more generous with a tip or tolerant of a late pizza from a kid struggling to keep up, for one thing. By the same token, what does it do to our relationships when we turn an "I-Thou" — like a marriage, for example — into an "I-It" — as in using the other partner for personal sexual release (even consensually) rather than taking sex as an opportunity to strengthen your bond, grow as a couple, and express mutual appreciation?

This, to me, is the ultimate form of the Gift of Distinction: Taking care that you see the most important people in your life, whether your spouse, your parents, your friends, your children, as intrinsically worthy beings, created in the Divine image, with ends and purposes all their own, rather than as means to your ends — social, financial, or sexual — as subjects rather than objects. Further, the Gift of Distinction invites us to be sensitive to the fact that everyone we encounter — bank teller, store clerk, or police officer writing you a ticket — is likewise created in the Divine image, inherently possessed of infinite value and dignity as such. The more we realize this, and the more we allow this realization to penetrate even the most instrumental and trivial of our encounters, how much more might we increase kindness, respect, and generosity in our world?

Where It Comes From

The Jewish dietary laws come from a handful of verses in the Torah, which are later parsed and interpreted at great length in the *Talmud* and medieval law codes. These laws first begin to take shape in the Book of Genesis, when God instructs Noah that no one should eat the flesh of a living animal, eat the meat of an animal that is found to have died on its own or was killed by another animal, or eat blood of any kind. From these we derive traditions for harvesting animals whereby to be fit to eat, an animal must be killed as quickly and painlessly as possible, and its blood must be removed as thoroughly as possible before its meat is cooked.

Later, in the Book of Exodus, we first get the rule about not cooking a kid in its mother's milk, which we interpret to mean not cooking any meat together with any dairy product, or even eating them together cold, like in a cold meat and cheese sandwich. Many reinforce this separation by even having two sets of cookware and two sets of dishes — one set for meat, one set for dairy — as an extra precaution to avoid mixing the two.

Finally, the Torah enumerates in Books of Leviticus (11:3-8) and Deuteronomy (14:12-18) the categories or species of animal which are considered fit for Jews to eat and which are not. Most famously, we don't eat pork or shellfish, but we also refrain from eating any sea life that doesn't have both fins and scales, as well as rodents, birds of prey — sorry, no Thanksgiving owl! — or any creepy-crawlies like reptiles, amphibians, or bugs of all sorts. Looks like I'm going to miss out on the latest craze in protein bars made out of crickets. Aw. Shucks.

The Distinction we make in refraining from speaking badly about others — *lashon hara* — comes from for the exhortation, "You shall not go up and down as a tale-bearer among your people," (Leviticus 19:16) as well as a story in the Book of Numbers where Miriam is caught bad-mouthing her brother Moses and is afflicted with skin disease that only goes away after Moses prays for her (Numbers 12:1-16). In fact, the classical Jewish understanding of all the passages in the *Tanakh* about people getting leprosy is not about leprosy *per se*; the word "leprosy" is actually a poor translation. Leprosy (aka Hansen's disease) is a contagious neurological condition with very different symptoms from those described in the Bible. Our sages believed that any person afflicted with this condition — a *metzora* in Hebrew — was experiencing a physical manifestation of the spiritual ill of gossip, or spreading a bad name for someone. They thought of the word *metzora* — one who suffers from this condition — as an acronym for *motzei shem ra* — one who spread a bad name or reputation. (*Zohar, Metzora* 55)

The definitive Jewish texts on this subject were written by a teacher named Rabbi Yisrael Meir Kagan. Rabbi Kagan published two books — *Hafetz Hayim* ("Desirer of Life") and *Shmirat HaLashon* ("Guarding the Tongue") — both in 1873, citing all the sources in the Torah about the serious nature of practicing Distinction in your speech and how to go about doing it.

Making Distinctions not to speak oppressively to someone — *ona'at devarim* — comes from the Talmud, in the tractate *Bava Metzia* ("The Middle Gate"). *Bava Metzia* is largely a work of commercial code; that is, the laws and customs of ethical conduct in business dealings, like making sure you have fair weights and measures in the marketplace and not putting your thumb on the scale when weighing something you're selling. Dropped into the middle of this discussion — the *Talmud* loves tangents — is a discussion that begins, "Just as it is possible to wrong someone in buying and selling, it is also possible to wrong someone with your words." (*Bava Metzia* 58b) The specific actions warned against in this passage include teasing a penitent person about past deeds, reminding someone who converted about their or their parents' past religious behavior, or verbally misleading someone in business, as in the examples of donkey drivers and Best Buy mentioned earlier.

One particularly poignant rule: "If someone is suffering torments or illness, or is in the tragic situation of burying their own children, do not speak to them like Job's friends spoke to Job: 'Is not your fear of God your confidence, and your hope the integrity of your ways? Please remember: whoever perished, being innocent?'" (Job 4:6-7) In other words, "If you are suffering, you probably deserve it." Yeah, this is something you *don't* say to someone fighting cancer or burying a child.

Regarding Distinction in our intimate relationships, the Scripture is full of sexual do's and don'ts. The subject is addressed twice in the Ten Commandments: First, "Do not commit adultery." (Exodus 20:14) The world adultery in this context does not mean all extramarital sex; rather, it refers specifically to having sex with someone who is already married to someone else. This is an important distinction: Practicing Distinction in sexual relationships includes refraining from interfering in other people's sexual relationships. It appears again in the prohibition on coveting: Do not covet your neighbor's house, his wife, his servants, his livestock, or anything else that is for him alone." (Exodus 20:14) Coveting is a tricky word here: In common English usage "to covet" means to want, desire, or crave — all internal states or emotions, and in general Judaism is much more interested in regulating action than internal states. The accepted Jewish definition of coveting, from the medieval rabbi and philosopher Maimonides, is not a type of thought, but rather is the action of attempting to convince someone to part with something of theirs you want, when you know they have no intention of parting with it.

Another commonly referenced source on Distinction in sexual relationships is found in Chapter 18 of the Book of Leviticus. This section prohibits such things as bestiality and incest, and it also appears to condemn homosexuality.

Controversy alert: I say "appears to" because while the verse "do not lie with a man as one lies with a woman" (Leviticus 18:22) is the most commonly cited proof text for condemning homosexual relationships and the sanctioning of LGBTQ identity and behavior in general, taken in context, I believe this interpretation misses the point of the overall passage entirely. All other verses in this section prohibit either coercive acts — an animal or a child in one's family cannot give informed consent, due to lack of understanding or a real power differential between the two parties — or acts that spoil another couple's intimate relationship. In this context many contemporary rabbis interpret the verse about two men lying together as prohibiting this act insofar as it is non-consensual or adulterous as was — and is — often the case. Some rabbis interpret this as specifically (and exclusively) prohibiting anal intercourse between men;

however, because it is possible for two men to be in a committed relationship without doing this specific thing, this verse should not imply that discriminating against people for sexual identity alone is permissible. Our understanding today of sexuality as being somewhat biologically determined, in the light of our overarching value of recognizing each person's inherent dignity as being created in the Divine image, precludes categorical rejection of another person's identity and how they act to strengthen a committed, consensual relationship. This is where I stand: As a rabbi, I welcome committed couples of all sorts into my community, and I will officiate weddings between two men or two women, provided I can tell they are committed to one another exclusively . . . and they are both Jewish. Not all rabbis agree with me on this, but I feel like you and I have been through enough so far in this book to earn some trust, and it's important to me that you know where I stand, even if it's controversial. You are free to disagree.

But much more important to me is your understanding of the broader principle expressed in this text: Healthy sexual relationships cannot be coercive, degrading, violent or meant to do harm to the sexual relationships of others. To do so would make an object of your sexual partner, rather than a subject with independent will and inherent dignity. The strong trend in the Jewish tradition is that sex is best in "I-Thou" relationships, and should be avoided in "I-It" contexts.

Where I Am

I mentioned that I have a favorite verse in the Torah: "Do not oppress the stranger . . ." (Exodus 23:9) I also have a favorite passage of Talmud, and it's the one cited earlier regarding *ona'at devarim* (speaking to someone in a hurtful or misleading way). So often the favorite things that we learn aren't just about the *content* of the teaching but also the *context* in which we learn them. In this case I was referred to this passage by a teacher of mine, Rabbi Elliot Dorff, not merely because of my intellectual curiosity, but because of a professional emergency. In my second year of rabbinical school I was serving as an on-campus chaplain at American Jewish University in Los Angeles, acting as rabbi for the undergraduate students of the school that housed my graduate seminary program. A student came to me one day, really upset about a recent spate of what we now call cyber-bullying: She was getting vicious texts from a classmate, making fun of her for various aspects of her identity. (I'll leave out the particular content, lest either party read this book and become embarrassed about it.) I was at a complete loss for how to deal with this as a rabbi, whose main job is to teach the Torah relevant to people's current experiences to help them flourish. But what could the Torah and our sages of past millennia possibly have to say about cyber-bullying, a uniquely 21st century phenomenon, enabled and accelerated by the advent of the internet and mobile phone technology?

I asked Rabbi Dorff, who was not only my teacher for several seminary classes, but also the Rector of American Jewish University and, in my opinion the greatest living scholar on the subjects of Jewish law, philosophy, and ethics. I hadn't seen him publish anything on cyber-bullying per se, but he is always on the forefront when it comes to the interface between technology and Jewish ethics. I didn't know what Rabbi Dorff would have to say about cyber-bullying, but I knew I could count on him for something wise and something appropriate to protecting the dignity of my students, and I wasn't disappointed.

He pointed me in the direction of the *Mishnah* on *ona'at devarim*, and I studied it as well as the passage of Talmud commenting on it, which is the text I mentioned earlier. I was aware of the prohibition on *lashon hara*, and I could surmise its implications on one form of cyber-bullying — talking badly about other people online — but would it address the possibly more insidious behavior of using digital technology to attack someone directly, even in private? For example, more recently there has been a trend among young people to message the acronym "KYS" to each other ("Kill Your Self") as a form of bullying, though this was not used in the interaction I'm talking about.

The answer came from our principle that speaking to another human being in a way that embarrasses them, whether in private or in public, is as grave a sin as spilling their blood. Once I felt I understood the text Rabbi Dorff gave me well enough to teach it, I brought it to teach each of the students involved in this cyber-attack, and a little later I convened a learning session with a larger group of my undergraduate charges, and we learned the text together. I don't know that the two students involved are exactly friends today, but the bullying stopped, and I didn't hear of another case of it among the undergrads for the rest of that year.

I also learned from this experience that there is perhaps no problem in human experience, whether old and inherent to the human condition or brand-new as a byproduct of cutting-edge technology, that can't be improved by the application of Jewish principles, such as the Gift of Distinction.

What to Do

1. Keep a food diary for six days.

Starting on the next Sunday, keep a diary of everything you eat for six consecutive days. Use any record keeping device you like: A notepad app in your smartphone, a real-live little notebook, a few index cards you keep in your wallet . . . whatever works best for you to keep a thorough log of everything you eat or drink (besides water). No need to adjust your diet at this point (although studies show that when people log their eating habits, they automatically eat less food, and what they do eat is healthier). After six days, Sunday through Friday, take Saturday off, eating as you wish, but not writing anything down. Then on the following Sunday, look through your diary. Take a pen or a marker and cross out (or on an electronic device, delete) anything that contains pork or shellfish. Look at your diary again. If you only ate what's left, would you be going hungry? Take one more pass through the list and highlight anything that has meat or poultry mixed in with dairy products. Ask yourself, if I changed this to have meat OR milk, instead of both, could I still enjoy it? The point of this exercise is not to make you feel judged, ashamed, or pressured into changing behavior; the point is for you to show yourself that it's possible to gain the confidence and pride of exercising spiritual discipline over the most human of activities, while also not starving death, and that doing so would be relatively easy.

2. Keep a speech diary for six days.

Once again, starting on a Sunday and going through Friday, keep daily score of how you communicate with and about people. This one's more specialized, and I recommend an index card and a golf pencil, but you do you. While doing you, do this: Over the course of each day, mark a letter X on the card every time you say something negative about someone else who's not in the room. For this diary, social media and email counts, too! Tweets or Facebook status updates that share gossip are still gossip. Any time you say, email, post, or tweet something critical about someone, even if it's true, even if you are their manager or a movie critic and it's your job to critique them, mark an X. Again, this exercise is about observing your own behavior, not modifying it (just yet). Likewise, every time you say something negative *to* someone, even if it's true, even if you think they deserve it, mark your card with the letter O. Do this Sunday through Friday, then take Saturday off. Unlike the food diary, I don't encourage you to gossip or criticize normally on your day off, but also like food journaling, you may find incidentally that your speech patterns have improved automatically, just by being more aware of them. Then, on the following Sunday, look at your Xs and Os. Are there certain days, or times of day, or special events, that contribute to an increase or decrease in this kind of talk? Did your letter-count go down as you became more aware of it? Once more, this exercise is about awareness, not shame.

3. Give yourself a relationship review.

This one won't take six days, but it might take several hours. See if you could block off a Sunday afternoon to do it in one or two sittings without too many interruptions. Once more, on a writing platform of your choice, make a list of everyone in your life you currently have a relationship with. Start close: Living family members, both the ones you live with and the ones you don't. If there are family members you know exist, but you haven't talk to them in years and don't plan to in years to come, you can leave them off; this is a list of people you know and interact with at least once every year or two. Next: Friends, the people you see socially at least once a year, if not every week. Include social media "friends" only if you have communicated with them one-on-one in the last year. Next: Work associates, all the people in your office, store, jobsite, polka band, etc. These can be your supervisors, direct reports, co-workers, customers you know by name, or current clients. You don't have to copy/paste your company directory or email contacts, but these might be a good place to go for a reminder of all the people you interact with on a regular basis. Another good resource might be your calendar; scan through it and list all the people you met with more than once in the last year. I warned you this might take a while, but in the end, I think it will be worth it. Last, round it out with the people for whom you are a client or customer: The postal carrier in your neighborhood, your kid's teachers, your mentors, your clarinet teacher, rabbi, pastor, relationship coach, or energy healer, anyone you interact with whom you know by name, even in passing. Once that list is made . . . Congratulations! That was a big job. Looking at the length of the list of people you interact with, you may have feelings — impressed, depressed, grateful, or overwhelmed. Do me a favor: Write down how you feel about that list in a sentence or two at the bottom of the list. Then take a break: You've earned it. Walk around the living room, or around the block, and massage your writing hand. I imagine the list was longer than you expected. Then, when you've had a good breather, or a nap, or a fortifying beverage of some sort, sit down with the list again, and do this: Recalling our discussion of "I-Thou" relationships (appreciative) and "I-It" relationships (instrumental), go down the list and mark a score for each name on a scale of 1 to 10 (1=purely instrumental, 10=purely appreciative). Here's a trick I heard from author Timothy Ferriss: Don't use 7. This is a cop-out number, one we choose as a passing grade to avoid true and perhaps painful evaluation; force yourself to choose between rounding up to 8 or down to 6. Once more, once you're done, take a look over the list, note your frequency of high-scorers and low-scorers. Then, take a moment to write a couple of more sentences at the bottom of your list how you feel about the results. Extra credit: If you're a real data nerd like I am (surprised? I was a financial analyst once), you can pop the list into a spreadsheet, get a grand total and an average score for benchmarking, and maybe do the exercise again in a few months, and see how the total and average change, once you've spent some more time being mindful of the quantity and quality of relationships in your life.

4. Take the One-on-One "I-Thou" challenge.

This is an exercise in appreciative inquiry, and it is a buddy exercise. You can do this with your study buddy from the Gift of Learning (that way you both get it done!), or it can be with a spouse, partner, friend, or someone else who will try something weird (but safe) with you without judgment. Go to a quiet place where you won't be disturbed or interrupted for 20 minutes, and if either of you has a mobile phone, put the phone in silent mode and out of reach for the duration of the exercise, unless you wish to use a phone as a timer. By the way, you'll need a timer. Take turns doing this: One of you talks for five minutes about an important moment that changed the course of your life or somehow strengthened who you are today. That person's job is to speak honestly. The other person's job is to listen without interrupting: They may nod, make facial expressions appropriate to what they are hearing, but may not say anything, only listen. Once the five minutes is up, the listener has two minutes to ask questions about what they heard — no statements, only questions — but the original speaker *may not answer them.* Just two minutes of unanswered follow-up questions. This may sound weird, and it will certainly feel weird when you do it, but trust me on this. Then, switch: The questioner tells a story for five minutes, and the original storyteller listens and then asks questions. After each of you has had a chance to speak, listen, and ask questions, reflect with one another how the exercise felt. What was it like to tell an important story without being interrupted? Did the questions make you feel like you were heard, and that the listener cared about what you were saying? Does the other person feel any more "real" to you now, as an end unto themselves, rather than a means to your end?

5. Host a Mindful Dinner Party.

This is a synthesis of the previous exercises, so do this last, once you've given at least some of the above a try. Host a gathering of some sort with food — dinner, a picnic, a back-yard barbeque — and invite six to 10 people. I suggest picking people from your Relationship Review list who are a mix of people you scored as 8s and 6s — people you appreciate, but would like to appreciate more, and people you recognize you could appreciate better than you do. Select the for the menu foods that are "fit" for a mindful diet — no pork or shellfish, no mixture of meat and milk, or you could go pure cruelty-free: vegetarian or vegan. If you don't want to do all the cooking or pizza-ordering yourself, consider making it potluck, giving your guests some dietary guidelines for a mindful/spiritual-themed dinner. When the party starts, thank everyone for coming, say some blessings or words of gratitude to the Source of the food, and dig in. After dinner, consider adding more words of blessing or gratitude, then invite your guests to pair up, and guide them through the appreciative listening exercise you did in Step 4, with you as the coach and timekeeper (and a participant, if you have an odd number of guests). If you invited any couples, you can choose whether to separate them for this exercise, or not; who knows, it could be healthy for a couple to be reminded of the power of appreciative listening. After the exercise is over, encourage people to relax and, if they want, share what they learned from the exercise. Before the evening is over, make sure you have spent some quality one-on-one time with your 6s.

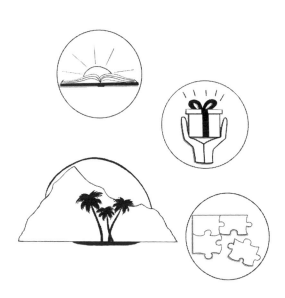

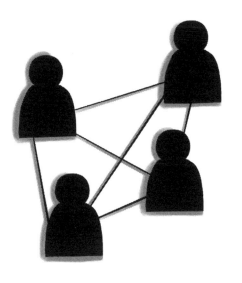

THE FOURTH GIFT
COMMUNITY

"If I'm not for myself, who will be for me?
But if I'm only for myself, what am I?
And if not now, when?"

— *Pirkei Avot* 1:14

"What should young people do with their lives today? Many things, obviously. But the most daring thing is to create stable communities in which the terrible disease of loneliness can be cured."

— Kurt Vonnegut Jr.

Sustainable personal growth requires social support. Sharing your path with others makes it more meaningful, enables more joy, provides greater human connection, and helps defend against one of the greatest public health threats of the 21st century: loneliness.

Where You Are

I'm writing this book in the United States of America in the early 21st century. The prevailing notion of identity here and now is the sovereign self: Each individual is primarily responsible for herself and to herself; if you are happy and successful, you get the credit, but if you are unhappy and unsuccessful, only you get the blame. The atomic unit of action, motivation, and rights is the individual. Occasionally, groups of individuals form coalitions to achieve a certain goal: to build a business, to win a football game, to elect a leader, or to hold a religious service. While people pitch in to varying degrees to accomplish that goal, each person walks home with his own reward — stock options, a Super Bowl ring, a politician that owes them personally, a warm fuzzy feeling about a caring universe that prizes himself above all. We are born alone, we die alone, and every achievement and failure in between are ultimately the prize or the fault of the individual, and every discussion of rights and responsibilities in this country, at this time in history, devolves to the rights and responsibilities of the individual in a free society comprised of approximately 325 million individuals, flying in formation.

And it sucks.

The downside of this "sovereign self" philosophy: Today, there is an epidemic of loneliness, and I use the word epidemic quite intentionally. Researchers compared the metrics of health and longevity of people who had strong social connections with people who did not, and they found something startling: Living alone, without frequent interaction with other human beings, has the same negative impact on one's life expectancy as, say, smoking cigarettes. Further, loneliness appears to be a self-reinforcing trap, a downward spiral: The less regular interaction with people you have, the more your social skills degrade, the less well-adjusted you are to interact with others . . . so the less likely it is that people to want to hang around with you. Spending a lot of time without company can make one angry and bitter, and so when people do come around to visit, they encounter an angry, bitter person, whom they are less likely to visit in the future.

I call this "bathrobe syndrome" — the more time you spend in a bathrobe, the more you look and act like someone who should spend more time in a bathrobe. I worked in the finance industry through the meltdown of 2008 and the layoffs that followed; I knew a lot of top financial executives who spent a year or more unemployed, holding out for jobs like the one they lost (often Chief Financial Officer-level positions). Trouble is, the longer they spent outside of an office, the less they looked like they belonged in the company of other people, so they increasingly went to job interviews wearing their executive best, but with attitudes and social skills that belonged in a bathrobe.

Where You Are Going

My advice to Bathrobe CFOs: Take a job, *any* job, that lets you be around people, and work your way back up. They had fallen into the loneliness trap, and it showed, no matter what they were wearing to the interview.

My second-best advice: Go to daily prayer services at your synagogue or church. Volunteer for some cause that puts you around people. Join a gym, but don't just put on the earbuds while you run on the treadmill by yourself; take an exercise class with other people. Build that social savvy back up, because I firmly believe that the Gift of Community — consciously putting yourself in the company of others, showing up and being there for others, and allowing them to be there for you, is a critical spiritual practice for living a happy, healthy life.

This is especially true if you are embarking on a new spiritual journey. You may have found this program by yourself, and you can (and must) do a lot of this work by yourself, and for yourself, but if you only do it alone, you will not reap the maximum benefit. In many ways, you may miss the point entirely.

Peter Berger, in his writing on the sociology of religions, coined the term "plausibility structures." A plausibility structure is an idea or set of ideas a person or group stipulates to be true as a basis for operation in the world. We have plausibility structures around gravity, which can't be seen, smelled, or heard, but the existence of which is faithfully verified every time we try to defy it. We have plausibility structures around love and relationships that lead us to act generously and faithfully with those whom we want to keep in our lives, hoping that they agree to this same plausibility structure, so as not to break our hearts. The standard ways of doing business in any company or industry — whether honest or cutthroat, whether cooperative or competitive or a judicious combination of the two — these rules of the game also form plausibility structures. Plausibility structures form the basis for every religion, as well as the reason for the splintering off of every single religious denomination.

The thing is, as Berger observes: Plausibility structures require social support. For such structures to endure, two or more people need to believe in them (or at least find them "plausible"), otherwise you risk crossing that fine line between common principles and individual delusion. You need to believe that other people (at least a few other people) believe what you believe. To sustain a practice, we need to believe that we are not only doing the right thing, but that other people believe we are doing the right thing as well. Otherwise, we begin to question our own sanity, or at least whether we are wasting our time.

In plainer terms: Whatever new practice or habit you want to integrate into your life, or whatever old pattern you want to reinforce, you will be more successful if you do it as part of a group.

Want to bowl regularly, and maybe even get better at it? You're better off joining a league than bowling alone.

Want to quit drinking alcohol or break another addiction? Alcoholics Anonymous and Weight Watchers figured out a long time ago that people are far more successful at breaking old habits and solidifying new ones in the regular company of peers and mentors on the same path, to offer support, accountability, and a little bit of positive peer pressure in the right direction, all of which makes growth and change far more likely to succeed.

Speaking of things people figured out a long time ago, it is perhaps for this reason that the Jewish tradition developed a practice of requiring a *minyan* (which means "counting" or "quorum") — a gathering of 10 or more people required for certain prayers to be said out loud. In communities where it's customary for adults to pray three times a day, and in a prayer-practice where the holiest prayers could only be said in a group, this pushed people to seek out prayer groups or *minyanim* in which to say their daily prayers, and this group became a supportive social network for its members as well. Showing up regularly is appreciated because you are also helping someone else fulfill their own duty to pray in a group, and if you didn't show up, you were missed.

Pop quiz: How many groups or places do you have in your own life right now — not including your immediate family or your workplace — where you feel appreciated just for showing up, and where people would miss you if you weren't around?

If you have such a group or place, you know how good that makes you feel. If you don't, you may know just how much harder life can be without it.

Another critical area where this Gift works to improve lives is in the process of mourning and bereavement. One tradition we have is that those who have lost someone close to them, like a spouse or immediate family member, are called upon to say a certain prayer — called *kaddish* — in honor of the deceased every day for a certain period: every day for a month if you've lost a sibling, spouse, or child, but every day for 11 months if you've lost a parent. The *kaddish* is one of those prayers that should be said in a group of 10 people or more. The strange thing is, the prayer itself contains no language about death, loss, or bereavement; it's about the exaltation and sanctification of God's Holy Name. The practice of mourners saying this prayer regularly is first observed in the 13th century CE, and my hypothesis is that our forebears started this practice not to give mourners an extra obligation or chore to do in their already difficult lives. I believe the practice started because it was and is a way to encourage people who are suffering to find a community so that they don't suffer alone, and it was and is a way to encourage the rest of us to embrace those who suffer with holy community at the time when they need it most.

Where It Comes From

So much of Jewish history and tradition is inseparable from community living. It's not hard to find particular sources, but it is hard to find a single source that does justice to the breadth and depth of the Gift of Community, because in the Jewish world, most of our literature of the past and our modern day-to-day, the existence of a tight-knit community and the knowledge of one's role in it is taken for granted. Nevertheless, Judaism and Jewishness has always been a people as much as it has been a faith or belief system, so our sages of the past had strong opinions about the value of community.

There are two teaching of Rabbi Hillel, a sage who taught about 2,000 years ago, that come to mind. The first reinforces both the necessity of self-regard and the essential connection an individual has to the community: "If I am not for myself, who will be for me? But if I am only for myself, what am I?" (*Pirkei Avot* 1:14) On the one hand, it's clear to Hillel that it's not necessary to totally disappear into community and give up all claims to one's self worth. Quite the opposite: We're enjoined to stick up for ourselves if we want anyone else to stick up for us, with the implication that community exists not to obliterate individuals, but to support them. On the other hand, Hillel believes that one who sticks up for himself alone, without sticking up for anyone else, isn't worth much. Rabbi Dorff points out in his teachings that compare traditional Jewish thought with contemporary American thought, Judaism doesn't place the same value on rugged individualism that is typical of the American myth of the lone hero, though the most successful people I know in America would quickly cop to the dual characteristics Hillel describes: They have succeeded beyond people's expectations because they believed in themselves when perhaps no one else did, but none would claim they got there without a team they had to nurture along the way, and who in turn lifted them up.

The other teaching of Hillel that pertains here: "Don't separate yourself from the community." (*Pirkei Avot* 2:5) Judaism makes heroes of its scholars, but there is almost zero mythology or history around hermitage. We don't have monks. Our greatest saints and scholars were immersed in community as teachers and leaders, but also as butchers and bakers and candlestick makers. There are certain prayers in our liturgy, considered the highest in holiness, that are not supposed to be said with fewer than 10 people present. I believe this custom itself arose from our sages' recognition of the individualistic impulse, even or especially in spiritual matters, so they decreed a couple of things: 1) You should pray regularly in three services a day; and 2) those prayer services ideally should be conducted in a group of 10 or more people. This means that even the most introverted hermit had to see other people at least three times a day. This is a powerful antidote to bathrobe syndrome.

But the tradition pushes us beyond the parochial regard for one's own townsfolk. We have a saying that appears several places in our sacred literature: "All of Israel is connected to one another." (*Shevuot* 39a) That is, all Jews are responsible for one another. This means that not only do Jews have communal responsibility for the other Jews in their town; we are each individually and all collectively responsible in some way for every other Jew on the planet. That doesn't mean that I have to take a week off work and fly around the world to help Shmulik in Lithuania change a flat tire, but I do have responsibility to contribute charitably to global organizations that benefit Shmulik. The flip-side of that, though, is that I know if I had a flat tire anywhere in the world, some Jew I've never met in that town would bend over backwards to help me out, simply because of our connection. Though when you think of it, bending over backward is a weird way to change a tire.

Where I Am

You might think that as a rabbi, I'm a bit biased toward encouraging people to join communities; it's kind of my job, and my bread and butter, to boot. But let me tell you about the power of togetherness in my life, from long before I became a rabbi; in fact, I would say the Gift of Community has had such an impact on my life, it's one of the main reasons I eventually became a rabbi: to help others find and build holy communities and reap the benefit of this Gift for themselves.

First off, early in my professional life, my family moved to another state a couple of times for my wife's career as an academic. We started in the Washington, D.C., area where we belonged to the synagogue my wife grew up in. After a couple of years there, we moved to Knoxville, Tennessee. My wife had an instant social network with her colleagues at the university, but I was hard pressed to make new friends while also hustling to make ends meet. Not too long after we arrived, having recently converted to Judaism, I decided to begin the practices of daily study and prayer (encapsulated in this book as the Gifts of Learning and Gratitude) by finding a synagogue with a daily prayer service. What I found was instant kinship and friendship with a small group of people from all walks of life, for whom being Jewish was possibly the only thing we had in common. This was the social network I needed to find my way around town, to have people to talk to outside of work, and within this group I was also encouraged to learn more about the prayers, and eventually I learned how to lead some of the prayers and chant from the Torah in public during our services.

Perhaps more important, when I didn't show up, people would always ask me later, "Where have you been?" What started for me as a random assortment of individuals with whom I had only an interest in Jewish prayer in common, became a place that I missed — and was missed — when I was absent.

OK, they all had one other obvious thing in common: Most of them were significantly older than me. I thought perhaps this was my inner hipsterism presenting itself: I was, after all, keenly interested in the somewhat opaque (to a modern outsider) practice of traditional Jewish prayer, and maybe only older people were into what I was into. Old soul, and all that. But what I didn't understand until years later: many Jewish people outside very large, very traditional communities don't prioritize the daily prayer service. It's largely the same demographic you'll observe at a daily Catholic Mass, for example. What prompts people to come back to the synagogue daily, after years of not doing so, is *kaddish*, because they have to, because they just lost someone, and they start coming daily to say that prayer with a group. But here's the trick: When their one-month- or 11-month-long obligation for the prayer is over, by that time they've made friends with people with whom have discovered something in common besides their Judaism or interest in prayer: They're all someone who has lost someone, and now, once a day or even three times a day, they get to spend a few holy moments with people who get it, *really* get it, what it's like to be a widow or an orphan like themselves. Without knowing it, I'd walked into an informal bereavement group; however, even though I didn't share that aspect of my life with them yet, I still found an instant community of people who missed me when I was gone and supported me when I was present.

A few years later, I felt the value of the Gift of Community once again. It was a few months after my first wife and I separated. I was deeply lonely, and around came the holiday of Passover, for which I expected to be alone. This was an especially difficult prospect to face. See, Passover is hands-down the most popular and widely-observed Jewish holiday; even Jewish people who have become completely secularized and assimilated, and don't observe any other Jewish holiday, tradition, or practice, will get together with family, friends, or both for a Passover *seder* — an elaborate sit-down dinner that is accompanied by a ritualized retelling of the story of Moses and the Hebrew slaves and their exodus from Egypt (found in the book of — you guessed it — Exodus).

If you have never experienced a Passover *seder*, first, imagine Thanksgiving dinner, with anywhere from 10 to 100 or more in attendance. The largest Passover *seder* in the world, run by Jewish emissaries in Kathmandu, Nepal, regularly seats over a thousand people in a hotel ballroom, but these dinners are usually held in a family home. Then, imagine that dinner takes four to six hours while all in attendance take turns recounting parts of the story of the first Thanksgiving of the Puritan immigrants to America, complete with rambling tangents, commentary, and endless argument about the details. Plus songs. Plus the ritual requirement for every adult to consume four cups of wine (at least) over the course of dinner. Four cups of wine rarely make anything go faster. Now, imagine it doubled: Many Jewish communities celebrate Passover and other biblical holidays for two days in a row! Dinner guests may include an entire extended family, or multiple extended families who take turns hosting, plus friends and friends of friends, plus any new boyfriend or girlfriend being vetted by the family; this is how I was invited to my first *seder*, with the woman who would be my first wife.

But fast forward a decade or so, and imagine spending the evening alone while your children celebrated this holiday, this no-holds-barred family extravaganza, at your in-laws without you.

As a convert, I had no Jewish family of my own to join for the holiday. We had moved to the area for my wife's studies less than two years before, and I usually worked long hours and didn't socialize much outside the family, so I didn't have a lot of connections to the local Jewish community. But it turns out, I didn't need a lot of connections: I only needed Sid. Sid is a friend of mine I met at the synagogue, during the brief weekday morning prayer services, which I'd begun attending again on the mornings I no longer had my boys to get to school. One morning, as Passover approached, Sid asked about my *seder* plans. I said I had none. Without pause, without checking with his wife, he said, "Would you like to join us?"

That question, in that moment, probably kept me connected to the Jewish community, at a time when my connection was most tenuous and frayed. It may have been the singular moment where one person's generosity of spirit (followed later by generosity of brisket) was most critical to my hanging on to something I felt slipping away. Because of the Gift of Community Sid gave me that Passover, I stayed connected. I may not be rabbi today if it weren't for that question and that Gift. Naturally, the following year, when I was dating the woman who is now my wife, Sid not only invited me, but insisted she join me — perhaps to be vetted, as it were, by my chosen family, or the family that chose me. She had never been to a Passover *seder* before. So I said to her, "First, imagine Thanksgiving dinner . . ."

But the time I felt the power of the Gift of Community most keenly was a few years later, and this time, I had lost someone.

It was about a year before I started rabbinical school. I had begun working with a college student to help me with my Hebrew. Entering the seminary required the equivalent of a year or so of college-level Hebrew, and I barely knew the Hebrew alphabet, like Akiva in the cave, minus a few years, and a consultant instead of a shepherd. I was on my way to a coffee shop in Minneapolis to meet with my tutor, when I got a phone call from my sister in Dallas. She had just gotten word that my brother had died in a car accident in the desert outside of Phoenix. I was stunned. This was the first time someone close to me had died, other than a grandparent. I didn't know what to do next, except I knew I needed to make travel arrangements right away, so I called my tutor and cancelled our appointment, letting her know I'd be traveling for my brother's funeral, and that I'd contact her to reschedule when I knew my own schedule better.

Now, I knew my tutor was Jewish, but I also knew she lived across the river in St. Paul and wasn't a member of my own synagogue or any other Jewish community or group I was involved in; as far as I knew, we didn't have a single mutual friend. So I was shocked that within 20 minutes of cancelling with her, I got a phone call from my rabbi.

"I heard about your brother, and I called to tell you I'm so sorry for your loss."

I didn't call him to tell him. He heard and called me. In the 20 minutes since calling my tutor, I hadn't talked to a single other person outside my family, all of whom lived in Dallas and didn't know my rabbi or even what synagogue I belonged to.

So this tutor, who barely knew me, must have called around the synagogues in my area, found out which one I belonged to, left word for the rabbi of a thousand-family congregation, and he dropped what he was doing to call me.

Then another phone call came in, also from my synagogue. I don't even remember who it was, except that it was someone I barely knew, but they had made a point of calling me and telling me how sorry they were for my loss.

Then another call, and then, within about an hour of me first telling my tutor about my brother's death, there was a knock on the door of my apartment.

It was a woman from my synagogue's Sisterhood — a women's club within the community — wearing a mournful, consoling smile, and holding a foil-wrapped *kugel* — a kind of dense noodle casserole, typical Jewish comfort food.

Now, whenever people ask me what the Jewish community is all about, I invariably start my answer with: "Three phone calls and a *kugel*." And that's only counting the phone calls I received; who knows how many more phone calls were made finding out who my rabbi was, mobilizing the community, and finding a volunteer to bring me that *kugel* post-haste.

Now, whenever I work with a student who is considering converting to Judaism, but has reservations about feeling alone and like an outsider, or whose parents are concerned for their safety joining a people who face occasional persecution, I tell them about my three phone calls and a *kugel*. No matter who you are or where you come from, as a Jew, you have people who care about you and will actively care for you. On the grander scale, if you're worried about your personal or communal safety, you can know that whatever person or empire takes a notion to harm you, as a Jew, you will have approximately 20 million people in the world who have your back. This, for me, is one of the keys to our people's remarkable endurance over millennia: our commitment to taking care of each other, our commitment to the Gift of Community.

What to Do

1. Do a Community History for yourself.

Make a list of all the different communities you have belonged to throughout your life. These could be towns, religious organizations, schools, bowling leagues, sports teams, condo associations, Eagle Scouts, Rotary clubs, marching bands, Meet-Ups, a PTA, or even a yoga class you attended long and often enough to make friends. Any group that gathered people with something geographic, mission-based, or hobby-related in common, for mutual support and fellowship. Feel free to include companies you've worked for or professional associations you've belonged to, provided they had more than two people and felt like a community. You can of course include online communities: Facebook groups, forums, Reddit subs, and the like if you sincerely feel you have cared about the people in the group and they have cared about you. (I'm a firm believer that an online community is a *real* community, when the people involved care about each other, even if they've never met in person.) Take your time. Look through old pictures albums if it helps, or your resume, or an online social network you belong to. If this is daunting, just give yourself 30 minutes to an hour to list all you can.

Then, like in your Relationship Review in the previous chapter, go down the list and rate them from 1 to 10, with 10 being your "happy place" and 1 being the worst place you could imagine ever going back to again. Once again, challenge yourself to not use the number 7; force yourself to not give any community a merely passing grade, but make it earn its place in your mind by rounding up to 8 or down to 6, as appropriate.

Below your list, take a moment to make another list. For the few places that scored the highest, list three to five things about them collectively that made them awesome. Then, for your low-scorers, list three to five things about them collectively that keep you from going back. The purpose of this exercise is for you to see just how many (or how few) tribes you have been a part of in your life, and maybe still are today. Very few of us, besides those in closed-off fundamentalist religious communities or those imprisoned in solitary confinement, belong to only one tribe anymore. In America especially, it's normal to belong to more than one tribe, and to have overlapping or differentiating tribes compared to your friends — the company you work for, the neighborhood you live in, the sports teams you root for — without too much conflict between tribes or between friends, and it's important to recognize that. Another outcome of this exercise is to get you thinking about the features of the communities you have loved, as well as the features of the communities you could live without. Having these pluses and minuses in mind, and maybe even written on a notecard in your purse or wallet, could be very handy in the next exercise.

2. Go "Shul Shopping."

"Shul Shopping" is what Jews call visiting multiple synagogues, looking for a "fit" before committing to one community long-term. (See the Glossary for an explanation of *shul*.) Preferably with your study buddy — though you can also do it alone if you must — sit down and come up with at least five but no more than seven different intentional communities you can visit within easy driving (or even walking) distance from your home. By intentional community, I mean a place where people regularly gather, at least monthly if not weekly or even daily, for a common purpose of greater meaning. For example: A synagogue, a church, an active yoga studio, a meditation group, perhaps a meet-up of vegetarians or atheists as long as it's regular, an Alcoholics Anonymous meeting if that's your jam, maybe even throw a SoulCycle or CrossFit class into the mix — anywhere people gather and meet regularly to support each other in pursuing a higher calling. Write down exactly when and where they meet, and make a plan to visit with your buddy each place at least once over the next month or two. Put it in your calendar, map it on Waze, whatever it takes to make sure you attend together. Schedule it, and schedule additional time afterwards to chat with the people in the community after the meeting or service, and also time right after that to meet with just your buddy to discuss the experience. Finally, when you're alone, write down a summary (or even fine detail) about the experience. What did you like about it, or not? Did it have the qualities you listed at the end of the previous exercise? Most importantly, would you go back?

After you've visited your whole list, check in with your buddy to see if they'd be willing to return to one of the places with you again at least once.

Note: If you already belong to a community like this, congratulations! I have no interest in your abandoning it. Please try the experiment anyway. At the very least, you will probably confirm for yourself, by contrast, what you like most about your community, but perhaps have begun taking for granted. And even if you love your current community, I think it's valuable to see what's happening elsewhere once in a while. You never know: You may come back with great ideas to help make the community you love even better!

3. Join a Helping Community.

Find a service organization where people work together to serve others *outside* that particular community. For example, Habitat for Humanity builds homes for people in critical need of affordable housing; it does not build houses for other Habitat for Humanity volunteers (although sometimes the housing recipients pitch in to help). It could be a single-issue cause-based organization, like a group that focuses on hunger or homelessness in your area. It could be a more broad-based organization that has a number of different activities or issues around a theme, like the local office of a political party. It could be a local chapter of a service club like Rotary or Kiwanis that help with many different causes in a particular locale. If you're having trouble picking one to try in your area, repeat the Shul Shopping exercise, only this time instead of intentional communities, look at communities with an "outward" helping focus versus an internal or "upward" spiritual focus. This is also a good exercise to do with your study buddy, but can be done solo, as long as you're jumping in and willing to work with new people. Commit to one day of service or one project; don't feel like you have to make a long-term commitment right away, unless you're really inspired to do so. Once more, if you are already part of such a community, don't quit it! You're not cheating on your favorite charity here; you are broadening your horizons, expanding your social network, and maybe getting a few good ideas to take back and improve your existing community.

4. Go "Virtual Shul Shopping."

Take a couple of hours and repeat either Exercise 2 or Exercise 3, only this time, look for it online. Search for intentional communities and service organizations like these with an online presence (and perhaps only an online presence). It could even be a forum for discussing the finer distinctions between practical special effects versus CGI in sci-fi horror moves. (Really? Just me?). Ask your friends (real and virtual) for recommendations, and try a few out. If you find one or more that interest you, I'm giving you limited permission to lurk (that is, observe without contributing) for no more than two days just to get a feel for the group, its standards, and its particular etiquette, then you must post! Give someone a shout out, a clapping-hands emoji, or something to show your support. And I do recommend you do this exercise with groups that have a general bent toward mutual support. For instance, I'm in a Facebook group dedicated to first-time authors sharing information about the processes and travails of the writing life and the publishing process, lifting each other up when we get discouraged, and cheering each other on as we reach and pass milestones on the journey. I'm not sure I would have been able to finish the book you are holding in your hands right now were it not for the support of this group, and it has also felt good to help other newbie authors the way many before have helped me. Like I said: Online community can be real community, when the care you get and give there is real. Try and find one for yourself.

5. Join *this* community!

OK, this may sound like a bit of a plug, but bear with me. I'm really excited to see what we can make happen together as more and more people read this book, and when those who are inspired or helped by it are able to meet each other, discuss the ideas in the book, what you've learned about the world and about yourself by working through the exercises, what insights you can share with each other, and what we can build together. If this book has inspired you at all, there's one thing you can do for me in return, and that is this: Join the movement of other people like you, get to know them, let them get to know you, and share this path that we're on, cheering successes, and supporting each other in struggles and stumbles. That's what community is about in my book (literally and figuratively), and if that's something that you and I can help create for others together, I would be incredibly happy, proud, and grateful to do that work with you.

All you have to do is flip to the back of this book and follow the instructions to join the Promised Life Tribe.

Once you sign up, you'll get an email with further instructions about how to join and interact with this community, and you'll get occasional emails after that about how to connect with this tribe online, how to take advantage of future opportunities to learn together, and possibly how to meet up in person with others in the tribe at a live event near you soon.

We're waiting for you!

THE FIFTH GIFT
INNER WORK

"The repentant stand where saints cannot reach."
— *Berakhot* 34b

"Anger is often what pain looks like when it shows itself in public."
— Krista Tippett

The Gift of Inner Work provides us with the core practice of self-improvement: An honest assessment of our destructive habits, of how we've let others down, of how we've let ourselves down, and what to do about it, including both seeking forgiveness and being generous in forgiving others. We have the ability to acknowledge our errors and weaknesses, accept responsibility for them, make amends, and reconstruct our lives in such a way that when faced with similar circumstances in the future, we are empowered to make healthier decisions.

Where You Are

Are you angry? About what? At whom?

It's possible that someone did something to you that hurt you, physically or emotionally or both. It was wrong what they did to you; you know it, and they should know it, too, but somehow the consequences for them just don't match up to the pain they caused you. It feels terribly unfair. Not only were you wronged, but the failure of the other person to own it and make amends, and the failure of the justice system or the universe or, say, God to balance the books by punishing this person in some way that is proportional to the pain you have suffered makes you feel invalidated, like you don't matter. This adds insult to injury and compounds your pain. One way people deal with pain is by feeling it and expressing it as anger.

It's possible you did something you wish you hadn't. Perhaps you hurt someone, or you let them down. Perhaps that someone is you: You are disappointed in your own behavior, because you know you are better than how you acted, or you know you are stronger than how you failed to act. And that eats at you. You grow to resent yourself; you grow angry at yourself. This kind of anger is the most insidious, the most toxic, because there's nowhere else for that poison to go. It builds. It infects. And it becomes infectious: The anger you feel at yourself, you take out on others, and then you feel guilty because deep down you sense the injustice of this, and you become ever more disappointed in yourself. Thus, the shame spiral continues.

Anger is a way of feeling in control of a situation that makes you feel powerless. Feeling angry with someone is a psychological way of engaging someone you may feel you have lost access to. Holding onto anger feels kind of like doing something about your pain. We all feel it. We all act on it. Anger is very popular.

But I could be wrong. Maybe you're not angry. Maybe you're just sad and disappointed by someone else's behavior, or at your own. But this sadness persists because the scales are still not balanced, there is still no justice, no consequence in proportion to the transgression, and the situation or relationship remains unresolved, so you remain sad. The longer you remain sad without the hope of resolution or reconciliation, the deeper you may sink into despair, into feeling that the world is permanently unjust, and this saps your hope for a future of wholeness and growth.

Of course, I could be wrong about that, too. I sincerely hope I am: I do not wish you to feel anger at others, and I most sincerely hope you do not go around feeling anger at yourself. That's the worst (he said from personal experience). I hope that you do not despair of the existence of justice in the world, that you have not given up on the possibility of feeling resolution in your relationships with others or feeling wholeness within yourself.

But I'm willing to bet you have bad habits or, perhaps better said, habits you wish you did not have. We all have habits — they are quite literally hard-wired into our brains — and most of us have at least one habit we wish we felt strong enough to break. For some, it's chemical dependence. For some, it's over-eating. For some, it's gossip, or complaining. But for all of us, the habits we have — good or bad — are usually perceived as so integral to who we are that we do them without thinking; we often catch ourselves doing them without remembering starting the action willfully or even consciously. And when those unconscious habitual acts conflict with our values or impair our relationships in some way, we feel guilty, and perhaps angry at ourselves, and we beat ourselves up. But the habits persist.

There are things you carry that you wish you could put down. Anger. Guilt. Maybe the bottle, or its ilk. Carrying heavy things around is something we usually associate with someone who is strong; maybe that's why you do it, because it beats the heck out of facing that you feel weak. But there is a way to gain strength, gain lightness, gain wholeness by putting down those burdens we carry and breaking the hold of those habits which carry us away. This is the Gift of Inner Work — the practice of forgiveness and of return to the right path.

Where You Will Be

I'm a big proponent of focusing your time and energy on your strengths and largely ignoring your weaknesses rather that working to fix or remediate them. For the most part, I think people don't need to be "fixed," and I view self-improvement largely as a process of accepting that we're good as we are, and that we still get to grow, rather than dwelling on our brokenness and spending all our time addressing our flaws at the expense of developing our talents and further polishing what makes us shine. Nevertheless, sometimes there are things that hold us back from growth, and spending time and energy dealing with those things and squaring them away can allow our growth to resume or accelerate.

Enter the Gift of Inner Work. I call it Inner Work because most of the other practices in this book focus on the outward, embodied actions you can take that happen to have a profound positive impact on your interior state and experience. What comes next the opposite: Inner Work begins with introspection and modifying how you think about and react to certain things, which then has an impact on your outward behavior, your relationships with other people, and the world you inhabit.

There are two main components to this Inner Work: self-improvement and forgiveness.

"Wait a minute," you might say, "isn't this whole book about self-improvement?"

It is, in the categorical sense (the section where you might find it in a book store). But this part is a deeper dive, and "self-improvement" is perhaps the most accessible label I can use to translate a very deep, complex, and profound Jewish practice, perhaps the most important practice in this whole book, which has the name in Hebrew: *Teshuvah*.

Teshuvah literally means "return," as in, return to the right path or return to one's higher principles. The closest theologically equivalent word from outside Judaism is "repentance"; however, the Jewish practice of *teshuvah* offers (and requires) so much more than simple absolution through confession. It requires an internal recognition of the gap between your behavior and your standard of behavior, an acceptance of your responsibility for that gap, and a plan for how to bridge the gap today, and how to avoid the gap given similar circumstances in the future. Beyond that, it requires actively making amends to others, whether it's people you've harmed, or God, or even yourself. Say you're sorry — even if you have to say it a few times before it's heard and accepted — and pay your debts.

That's a lot of requirements. What does *teshuvah* offer? Nothing short of tremendous personal growth: New habits, improved character, possibly a new path to a bright future, or even better, a return to the good path you were on before.

Teshuvah is a way of making up for something you did wrong once, whether you failed another person, failed

God (or your concept of God, the higher authority you are responsible to), or failed yourself — harming yourself in the process or perhaps betraying your own standards and ideals. But *teshuvah* is not only for one-offs: It can also be effective for breaking habits of yours that are disappointing to you or disappointing to others. There's a place in Los Angeles called *Beit T'Shuvah* (Hebrew for "House of Return") that is a residential addiction recovery center. They have helped hundreds of people face and work through addiction to things ranging from drugs and alcohol, to gambling and gang involvement, to internet pornography, and they do it with an approach that combines the Twelve Steps of Alcoholics Anonymous, psychotherapy, and good old-fashioned traditional Jewish practice of *teshuvah*.

Charles Duhigg, in his book *The Power of Habit*, makes two powerful points about the formation and alteration of habits. First, neuroscientists have discovered that habits we form become embedded so deep in the brain — programmed into the oldest part of the brain, evolution-wise, the part we have in common with modern-day lizards — that they are nearly impossible to simply quit doing, because they become instinctive, carried out without conscious thought. Second, all habits are made up of a predictable recipe of cue, routine, and reward, in that order. A cue occurs, our lizard-brain responds with a programmed routine, and the routine elicits a reward that reinforces the habit. While it is, as I said, nearly impossible to remove a habit, it is relatively simple, if not always easy, to hack the habit; once you've recognized the cues that initiate the habitual behavior, you can substitute the unwanted routine with a healthier one, as long as there is an equally desirable reward at the end of the new routine. The example Duhigg gives in his book was a habit he had of taking a break every afternoon at a certain time to go to the cafeteria to get a cookie, a habit that was slowly adding pounds to his waistline. After analyzing the behavior, he realized that it wasn't really the calories he was after, but the company of the people he met in the cafeteria, so when the afternoon blood-sugar drop signaled cookie time, instead of going to the cafeteria, he went to someone's office and chatted with them for a few minutes. Same cue, new routine, same social reward, and a healthier habit.

As you work through the exercises at the end of this chapter, I invite you to consider what habits you'd like to change, and what habits you might like to replace them with, following this cue-routine-reward recipe.

The flip side of Inner Work, the complement to asking for forgiveness, is granting it. For one thing, there is great benefit to your psychological and even physical health when you lay down the heavy burden of any grudge you are carrying. There's an old saying: "When you hold a grudge, it is like drinking poison with the hope that it will make someone else sick." Second, when you forgive, you emulate the Holy One (if you're into that sort of thing). Third, when you forgive, you are encouraging people to do their own Inner Work, letting them know that if they are willing to do the brave work of *teshuvah*, you are willing to hear them out and reward them with your openness. You become an agent in their Inner Work, and when you put that kind of mojo into the world, you may find the world more receptive to your own Inner Work. You teach the other person not only about the quality of forgiveness; you also reward their courage in asking for it. Even if you don't believe you're responsible for the act or habit that damaged the relationship in the first place, you take responsibility for repairing it, you reduce the overall level of cruelty in the world, and you remove roadblocks to others' growth as well as your own.

Where It Comes From

Our tradition has it that *teshuvah* was created even before the material world:

> "Repentance was created before the world was created, as it is written: 'Before the mountains were brought forth, or ever You had formed the earth and the world, even from everlasting to everlasting, You are God' (Psalms 90:2), and it is written immediately afterward: 'You return man to contrition; and You say: Repent, children of man'" (Psalms 90:3).
>
> — *Nedarim* 39b

Our sages reasoned that before people ever walked the earth and began to act and interact, they needed a vehicle for expiation. Knowing none of us is perfect, it is comforting to know that we are a part of a fault-tolerant system, and we all have (and have always had, since before the dawn of time) a means to make amends with God and with each other. We need to know we can get better, we can be better — not better than anyone else, but better than we are today. We can heal, and we can repair. None of us is perfect, but all of us are perfectible. We have the technology.

One of our teachers of this technology was Maimonides. In his book, *Laws of Repentance*, part of a larger legal collection called the *Mishneh Torah*, Maimonides addresses both *teshuvah* (repentance) and *mehilah* (forgiveness). First, he distinguishes between a transgression between humans and God, versus a transgression between two humans. A transgression against God entails failure or error in keeping such religious precepts as the dietary laws, distancing oneself from ritual impurities like contact with a dead body, and the practice of offering agricultural sacrifices, and later, prayers which were structured to model the sacrifices. If you made an error here, no person was harmed *per se*, but the covenant between God and humans was marred and need to be corrected. This is accomplished through prayer, repentance, charitable giving, and self-affliction by means such as fasting. Though this can be accomplished any time of year, the Jewish holiday of Yom Kippur (Day of Atonement) is dedicated specifically to this kind of repair of the relationship between people and God. Maimonides notes, however, that while Yom Kippur and the kind of pious activity it represents is sufficient for "vertical" atonement, "lateral" atonement — that is, repair in relationships damaged by our transgressions against one another — requires making amends person-to-person. This personal order of reparation is not considered a lesser order, as we are each created in the Divine image. Maimonides considers interpersonal atonement as equally important in God's eyes; an insult or injury to any of God's creatures is an insult to their Creator.

That is to say, if you harm a person, prayer and fasting alone don't cut it: You have to make personal reparations before God will accept your plea of atonement. If you steal from someone or damage their property, you have to make them whole. If you insult them or embarrass them, you have to make amends and ask for their forgiveness. According to Maimonides, they have to forgive you before God will.

There are limits to this, of course; some people are slow to forgive. If you attempt to make amends three times, in the presence of witnesses, and the person still doesn't forgive you, you are considered absolved, and they are considered cruel. This brings us to the counterpart of repentance: Forgiveness. Being forgiving is more than just the avoidance of cruelty. It is considered Godly behavior, an act of honorable imitation. Just as the Holy One forgives transgression, so too must we forgive transgression. Just as God is merciful to us, so too should we be merciful to one another. Furthermore, acting with forgiveness is self-reinforcing. First, it teaches others that if they have the courage to make amends, their courage will be rewarded with acceptance, and they become more likely to make amends in the future. Second, by demonstrating forgiveness to others, you encourage them to be forgiving toward you when it's your turn to make amends.

In addition to being a scholar and a philosopher, Maimonides was also a physician. In 1198 CE he wrote his *Regimen of Health*, a treatise on hygiene, for an Egyptian sultan named Afdal Nur al-Din Ali. The sultan suffered from both physical and psychological distress at various times; Maimonides saw that these were interconnected, and he believed both could be addressed though hygiene — breaking bad habits and forming good habits. Over 800 years ago, he advocated for regular exercise, a high-fiber diet, and stress-reduction prescriptions such as lavender oil (known to have a soothing effect in aromatherapy today), to maintain a good mood and good mental health, and he believed that lowering stress in this way helped defend against physical afflictions as well. All of these recommendations remain common doctors' orders for mental and physical well-being today.

Where I Am

This is a story about my *teshuvah*, but it is also about someone else's. For the sake of not embarrassing another person (see: the Gift of Distinction), I'm going to change his name to Hank. In this story, I'm still John.

My friend Hank is 95 years old. If you do not have any 95-year-old friends, take my advice: Get some. I have at least three right now, and these are some of the most amusing and rewarding relationships in my life. In my social realm — primarily the Jewish community of Los Angeles — the 95-year-olds are usually WWII vets from back East who settled here after the war, or the California girls they married when they got here, or else they are Holocaust survivors who made their way with hope and resolution to the land of sunshine, orange trees, and movie stars. They live in modest houses they bought 60 or 70 years ago for $15,000 and could now sell today for around $1 million. All these people have an incredible attitude and perspective, and they are, by and large, unflappable. They've lived through every major upheaval this country has seen since the Great Depression. They worry about their health and mortality, but more often they worry about not being there for people they care about when they die. Best of all, they do not sweat the small stuff, and no one has more gratitude for each new day of life. If you want to have the optimal outlook on life, pretend you are 95.

I teach a class in my synagogue, one day a week in the middle of the day, so my students are largely seniors and retirees. One summer, I was teaching about the section of the Torah that discusses the rules about making vows (Chapter 30 in the Book of Numbers). In short, vows — specifically vows that invoke the name of God, as in "I swear to God that . . ." — are a serious business, and should be taken seriously, or else avoided altogether. Anytime you make God a counterparty to an arrangement, if you don't keep your end of the bargain, it's not just you that looks bad; you make God look bad. This is why some religious groups in America and elsewhere avoid vows and oaths in the civic sphere, as in during legal testimony; Quakers, for example, do not make vows or swear oaths, but will "affirm" the fidelity of their testimony in settings that require it. This is also the source of a common Jewish colloquialism, "*bli neder*" (Hebrew for "without a vow"), that some religiously serious Jews will throw into their speech whenever making commitments about the future, even the most trivial, as in, "I'll see you at the coffee shop at 2 p.m., *bli neder.*" This is not because we are untrustworthy or ambivalent about our interpersonal commitments. It is because we take the prohibition on vows so seriously, we take the honor of God so seriously, and we have such strong faith that everything is up to God and not to us, that we avoid any appearance of making vows that might dishonor God if something unforeseen comes up, like bad traffic, even for something as trivial as a coffee date.

So I was teaching my seniors about vows, and the conversation meandered somehow toward children, childrearing, and parental discipline. I mentioned that in my household, children would occasionally get a corrective *potch* — a Yiddish word for a spanking or a firm pat on the bottom when misbehavior occurred.

Now, I know I might have just lost you. Corporal punishment of children is a controversial subject. Some people take its necessity and effectiveness for granted; others see any hint or suggestion of it as child abuse, plain and simple. In my experience, good people disagree about this, in Jewish communities as in all communities. But in that room, while some of my 95-year-old friends nodded in recognition and recall of how they raised their own children (now in their 70s), Hank turned on me, at once turning pale and sitting straight up. "Rabbi," he said with shame and incredulity, "you mean to tell me you beat your children? *My* rabbi beats his children?!"

I explained that no, I do not beat my children, but I would administer the occasional corrective pat on the bottom when I thought nothing else will get their attention. Hank was having none of it. "If you raise your hand to your child in violence in any way, you don't know what you are doing, you don't know what effect that has on a child. You are crushing their spirit. You are making them fearful. You are abusing them!"

I attempted to diffuse his anger and defend myself at the same time, noting that I have a friend who is a pediatric psychiatrist and says, "Sometimes, kids need a *potch*." Hank would have none of it.

"Swear to me you will never raise your hand to your children, those precious little children, ever again."

Now he was really putting me on the spot. First off, we were in a room with about eight other people, most of them senior citizens whose respect I had earned over a number of years as the rabbi of their synagogue. This was a public challenge in front of people whom I wanted to continue to think well of me and trust me as a leader and as a teacher. Second, I had just taught a lesson on how we avoid swearing a vow if we think there's any chance we might slip, because it would dishonor God.

"Swear to me," he repeated. "Make a vow."

"Hank," I pleaded, "I'm not going to make a vow. I just told you, we don't do that. If I mess up, it's a violation against God."

"Hitting your kids is a violation against God." He had my number. "Swear it."

All eyes in the room were on me. But I couldn't look away from the bloodshot eyes of a 95-year-old man, because I saw, in their depths, that he knew exactly what he was talking about. What had he seen? What had happened to him? This shook me to my core.

"I swear," I said, timidly. Not my usual, booming, authoritative rabbi/teacher voice.

"Swear to God!" he said.

"I swear to God."

In that moment I felt like I failed as a teacher — to remain aloof, remain objective, get across the point that Jews shouldn't say "swear to God" lightly. My lesson got hijacked, and I'd lost control. But that wasn't the strongest failure I felt that day, and as Hank taught me, there are worse kinds of losing control.

A few months later, I was visiting Hank at home. Hank was under hospice care; age had caught up to various systems in his body, to the point where treating an ailment in one part could create any number of complications in other parts, so his doctor decided to focus Hank's care on comfort rather than cure. We'd had several conversations about death: what comes after for him, and what comes after for those he leaves behind. If he was afraid of dying for his own sake, of what would happen to him, he hid it well. What he did let show was his fear for his loved ones. Who would take care of them? A few visits in, he did allow himself to wax introspective.

"Rabbi, what's it all been for?" Hank asked me. "What difference have I made? Was the world any better because I was in it?"

One thing I knew about Hank: He considered himself a realist. He didn't go in much for God talk, or heaven, angels, spirit, eternity, or as he might put it, "that kind of crap." We'd had many debates in our mid-day lessons; whenever I'd share what the sages of our tradition thought about God's intention in a particular passage of the Torah, or the career of the soul before inhabiting the body and after, he'd bring me back down to earth. "God, or whatever you call it, doesn't care about us. Look at the Holocaust, look at the suffering, and what not. What does this fairy tale have to do with me? How does this make me a better person?" In these later visits in his home, or in the hospital, Hank shared less concern about what was happening next and more concern over who and what he was leaving behind. Who cares about the World to Come? What was his legacy in this world?

"You've raised a pretty great family, Hank," I said. "You've been a leader in our synagogue, and you've supported it for a long time. And I can't tell you what you've meant to me."

"Why don't you try?" he said with a special smirk you can only accomplish with your dentures out. There's no smart-aleck like a 95-year-old smart-aleck, because they've seen the most. They've earned the right to put you in your place. They know it, and you better know it, too.

"I'm a better rabbi for having known you," I said. "I remember the first time we learned from the Torah together. I had just started teaching Lunch and Learn," my weekly mid-day class, "and you asked me some hardball question about what I was teaching, and I used a classic teacher's dodge. 'That's a good question, Hank.' Which is what rabbis say when we don't know the answer, and we want to stall for time while we make something up. You put me in my place right quick. You said, 'I know. I only ask good questions.'"

Hank grinned. "I remember that."

"I haven't used that stalling tactic since," I continued. "You've made me a better teacher. But more than that, you've made me a better man. I've treasured our friendship, and I'll remember you as long as I live."

Never one to allow a conversation to remain grave, Hank said, "Well, thanks a lot, Rabbi." He adjusted his breathing tube in such a way as to make present and obvious the state of his health, and he said with mock-seriousness, "I'll remember you as long as I live, too."

We both cracked up. Sorry, not sorry. I hadn't laughed like that in a while, and clearly, neither had he.

"So, Rabbi," he gathered himself, "you said I made you a better man. How so?"

Our mirth had drawn an audience; his wife and one of his daughters were in the room now. Here he goes again, putting me on the spot in front of people. But he'd earned a good answer. After all, he only asks good questions.

"Since that day you put me on the spot about spanking my kids," I said, "I haven't done it once. Not one time."

His daughter spoke up. "What's he talking about, Pop?"

I told her about the time he put me on the spot in class, and he made me swear never to lay a hand on my children again. After I finished, she looked from me to her father.

"That's really something, you know, because, he didn't always feel that way." She wiped the corner of one eye.

A few beats of silence passed as she and I looked at Hank. Then he took a deep breath, rattling a bit on the exhale, as congestive heart failure was slowly filling his lungs with fluid. Then he told me a story. He told me of a time when his one son was a teenager, and had mouthed off to him. Hank hit him across the face so hard it knocked him to the ground. A hit like that isn't usually the first time you hit someone, but in this case, it was the last. Hank confessed that as soon as that had happened, the moment he saw his own son crumpled on the ground, hands raised in defense against the next blow, something in him broke, some part of the sense of himself as a man, as a father who is supposed to protect and nurture. He looked at what he had done, and he realized he should never do it again.

"I don't know if I'll ever make up for that, Rabbi. I don't know that I can make *teshuvah* for that."

"Whether you've made amends fully with your son," I said, "is between you and your son. I suspect you have. But that's not all there is to *teshuvah*. Another important part of it is, if you were faced with the same circumstances again, would you make the same mistake? I suspect you would not.

"But more than that," I said, "and this is above and beyond normal *teshuvah*: Not only did you stop making that mistake; you stopped me from making it, and God willing, my kids after me won't make it either, and so on. That's *teshuvah*, and something else. That's a legacy you can be proud of."

When you make *teshuvah*, when you reach deep down to make amends, fix broken relationships, and improve yourself, you teach others to do the same.

When you set the example of forgiveness, you inspire others to be forgiving, and the world becomes, bit by bit and thanks to you, a more forgiving place.

And that's a legacy you can be proud of.

What to Do

1. Find a partner for your Inner Work.

We talked before, regarding the Gift of Community, about plausibility structures requiring social support. Social support is also essential to changing habits, and many things we are trying to face in this Inner Work involve habits; we often find ourselves making amends for things we do repeatedly, and sometimes it is deeply ingrained habit that makes it so difficult to stop, much less envision a future when, if faced with similar cues, we'd run a different routine. In *The Power of Habit,* Duhigg points to the success Alcoholics Anonymous, and he admits that the program itself is a bit of a mystery to psychologists and other scientists who study addiction. Though the program isn't perfect — no one in it claims to be "cured" of their drinking habit — it has worked to prevent habitual drinkers from drinking, and no one in the scientific community knows exactly how it works as well as it does. What many agree on, however, is that the aspect of peer support is essential to success, both in the form of attending regular meetings as well as working with a sponsor who is also in recovery, just as it is often peer "support" that reinforces the bad habit in the first place. Your task: Enlist someone you trust to be your partner in self-improvement, and offer to serve as their partner in return. Agree that you will complete the following exercises together, without judgement, and with total confidentiality. This could be your study buddy, or it could be someone else. As you will learn a lot about one another, remember one of the principles of avoiding *ona'at devarim*: One must not embarrass a repentant person by reminding her of her former deeds that she is working to amend. Not only will doing Inner Work with a buddy improve your odds of success; this could develop a new or existing friendship into a near-unbreakable bond of mutual appreciation, accountability, and support.

2. Make a list of people who have hurt you. Forgive them.

Again with the lists! This is important work to do to clear the decks before you begin doing your own Inner

Work. Inner Work takes having some room in your consciousness to move around in, so before you start, you have to evict the people who are taking up space because you are holding a grudge. First, make a list of people who have harmed you in ways you are still mad about. Consider: Family, friends, frenemies, co-workers or people you go to school with, sales clerks, tradespeople, or other vendors, the guy who cut you off in traffic on your way to the bookstore to purchase this book, anyone who has disappointed you in a way that you still carry and relive whenever you think of them. Take your time with this list, and feel free to return to it when you remember or encounter others who belong there. Once you feel "done" (for now) go down the list and, once more rate them from 1 (mild inconvenience) to 10 (mortal enemy), and again try to avoid using the number 7. This time, I want you to start with the easy ones (literally, the 1s), and resolve to spend a few minutes each day actively imagining forgiving one new person each day, gradually working up the list toward those who are harder and harder to forgive. In the beginning of each session, go back and look at some of the names you may have crossed off . . . Do you still feel like you've fully forgiven them? If not, spend a few moments and try again. So far, all this forgiveness is internal and meditative; you have not actually, verbally forgiven anyone. That is as it should be, for now. I want to challenge you to take your time mentally rehearsing forgiveness toward each person on your list, until you feel totally confident that you are able to let go of the transgression, before you approach any one of them to offer forgiveness. The offer may not be necessary; they may not ask, or you may be out of touch. Jewish custom does not require us to forgive people who don't ask for forgiveness; nevertheless, your psychological and emotional health can get a big boost out of letting your grudges go. If you feel it will be healing to grant forgiveness to someone verbally, even if they don't ask, you may do so, but be careful about embarrassing them or opening old wounds in yourself. Forgiveness is more often a process than an instant resolution, more often a journey than a destination, so remember to forgive yourself if forgiving others takes time and trial to get it right.

3. Make a list of people you have hurt, with whom you have no resolution. Get resolution.

Now that you've done the important work of forgiving others, prepare to seek forgiveness for yourself. In a similar fashion to the prior exercise, make a list of people you need to ask for forgiveness. Run through the usual suspects: Family, friends (especially where the friendship is strained), co-workers or schoolmates, neighbors, people at the gym or at your place of worship, baristas you may habitually under-tip. Rank them from 1 (a small slight) to 10 (you're dead to them), skipping 7. Once more, start easy. *Teshuvah* takes strength, and growing in strength benefits from a slow build. But unlike forgiveness, this time it's not enough to ask for it in your heart. There is the Inner Work of recognizing what you've done, resolving not to do it again, and strategizing how to avoid making the same mistake in the future; however, for *teshuvah* to be completely effective, you are not considered successful until you've asked for forgiveness and offered to make amends sincerely at least once. If you wish to follow the Jewish practice, anyone who doesn't grant you forgiveness should be asked again, in front of witnesses (take your *teshuvah* buddy) at least a couple of more times. If you've done all this, and forgiveness is not forthcoming, be satisfied that you did the best you could, and move on to the next person. Because none of us is perfect, the list may grow from time to time, and clearing the list may be a life's work, but it's work worth doing for a life worth living.

4. Make a list of habits, routines, and weaknesses you are not proud of. Accept them, or make a plan to fix them.

Make a list of things you wish you could say you didn't do regularly, or at all, for example: Smoking, biting your nails, complaining. Then, rank them from 1 (no big deal) to 10 (ruining or shortening your life), skipping the number 7. Take your top few habits you'd like to break, and learn to recognize the cues. It might be helpful to take a notecard around with you, and every time you engage in the activity you want to get rid of in a given day, mark it down. The next day, do the same thing, only make a little note about what happened right before you felt like doing it. You will probably see a pattern emerge — maybe you only bite your nails while you're on the phone with your mother, or you always smoke right after a meal) — that's your cue! Then ask yourself what you get out of the habitual action. What's your reward? Make a note of the cue and reward for each of the habits you'd like to fix; understanding cues and rewards to habit is half the battle. What's left is to identity the routine in between the cue and the reward — the behavior you'd like to stop — and replacing it with another routine. Replacing the routine with another, healthier routine will be more effective in getting rid of the old habit than simply going cold turkey. You are likely to encounter the same cues, so give yourself alternative routines and rewards to cope with them.

5. Imagine habits, routines, and strengths you aspire to. Invite them into your life.

This can be integrated into Exercise 4; often to break bad habits, the most effective way is to reprogram with good habits, by just dropping a new routine in into the habit loop between the cue and the reward. First, make a list of things you wish you could say you did regularly: Exercise, eat more healthfully, spend more time with loved ones, or make a habit out of any (or all!) of the Gifts in this book. You could even rank them, 1 (meh) to 10 (yay!), skipping the number 7. Now imagine: what from your "good habit" list could you sub in right after that bad habit cue? For example, if you bite your nails during a scary movie, what if you did sit-ups instead? (Pro-tip: Ghosts are repelled by killer abs, I've heard.) If you smoke after a meal, try saying a blessing or taking a meditative moment. But I don't recommend sit-ups after a big meal. Trust me on this one.

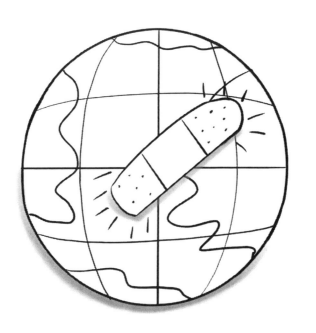

THE SIXTH GIFT
OUTER WORK

"Our rabbis taught: Deeds of kindness are superior to charity in three respects. Charity can be accomplished only with money; deeds of kindness can be accomplished through personal involvement as well as with money. Charity can be given only to the poor; deeds of kindness can be done for both rich and poor. Charity applies only to the living; deeds of kindness apply to both the living and the dead."

— *Sukkah* 49b

"How wonderful it is that nobody need wait a single moment before starting to improve the world."
— Anne Frank

This Gift invites us to pivot from a focus on self-improvement (Inner Work) to a focus on world-improvement (Outer Work). The Gift of Outer Work provides the core practice for achieving the sense of living a meaningful life, by finding activities and avocations that not only serve a cause greater than ourselves, but also that we really enjoy doing. Serving others and having fun doing it are the key ingredients of meaningful experience, and meaningful experiences are the ingredients of a meaningful life.

Where You Are

We've been learning together for a little while now, covered a lot of ground together, and by now I feel like our relationship is solid enough that I can take a risk and ask a personal question.

Have you ever felt depressed? By which I mean: Have you ever felt down in the dumps and despondent, like an outsider in your own life, and maybe you didn't even know why? I understand first-hand that clinical depression has a biological component to it, an imbalance or deficit in how neurotransmitters — chemical message-carrying molecules in our brains — are sent and received, and that these imbalances can be managed (if not cured) by medication. I also understand first-hand that depression can also be brought on by traumatic events, such as job loss, divorce, or the death of a loved one. But there is a third and, I'm willing to bet, more pervasive source of depression at play today. It's not chemical, and it's not necessarily event-driven. It's existential.

What do I mean by that?

Have you ever spent a significant amount of time — like several days in a row, or weeks (some of us, like me: years) — wondering if there was any point to your life, wondering whether your life has a purpose? Wondering *why* you exist?

Look, if you haven't . . . that's cool. Mazal tov. But if you have, and if these thoughts have plagued you to the point of distraction, then you, my friend, have experienced what's known in the biz as an Existential Crisis. Perfectly normal, perfectly healthy (depending on how you respond to it).

The Existential Crisis is an affliction that's been around forever, but its incidence and effects are greater now than ever. In the mid- to late-20th century it was commonly expressed and understood as the Midlife Crisis, when middle-aged men with decent jobs and established households would buy a red sports car, perhaps run off with younger women, and engage in other risk-seeking or attention-seeking behavior, or develop a serious substance-abuse problem to cope with the pain and dissonance. In the late 20th and early 21st centuries, someone coined the term "quarter-life crisis" to describe the experience of Gen Xers hitting a wall in their late 20s and early 30s, wondering if they'd made a mistake in choosing their career or lifestyle. Those in crisis would then often go back to school to retrain for another career. (This guy.)

I believe these "something-life crises" come from the same source, and are all really manifestations of the Existential Crisis: what happens when someone is faced with the question of what their life is really all about. And more: What is human life really all about? Why does the world exist, and what's my proper role in it? Why am I here, what is my purpose, what is "the point" of my life, and what do I do if I missed "the point" all this time?

Again, I don't know if you've ever had these questions. I suspect that if you're reading this book, you have, and I'm here to tell you that you're not wrong, weird, or broken for asking them (or any more wrong, weird, or broken than the rest of us). All advice is autobiography, so all I can tell you is that I've been there, too. I've worked through it, and I continue to work through it. I don't have all the answers for everyone, everywhere, but I have my answer, and I share it here in case it helps you.

My answer? Service. As in: service to others, not a religious service at a house of worship, but serving other people, or serving a cause greater than yourself.

Where You Are Going

The essence of Outer Work is marshaling what resources you have, what talents and desires and aspirations you have been given or have accumulated over time, and using them to help other people, to help the world.

Now, don't freak out. You don't have be Mother Teresa. You don't have to sell all your possessions and give the proceeds to the needy while you wear burlap and live in a monastery. You don't have to quit your job and join the Peace Corps (but who knows: maybe deep down, you want to). All you have to do is think outside the box a little, to see that in addition to taking care of yourself as best you can by working on your own personal growth with the other Gifts in this book, you can also contribute to the growth and well-being of others. And you can have fun doing it!

So I'll extend my answer a little: Service . . . with a smile.

Philosopher Susan Wolf, in her book *Meaning in Life and Why It Matters*, did not attempt to answer the question, as many philosophers have, "What is the meaning of life?" Instead, she asked the question, "What do we mean when we describe life as meaningful?" She wondered about the components, ingredients, or specific actions that let us look back on an experience and say,

"That was a meaningful experience," or "I feel like I live a meaningful life." Her conclusion: Meaningful experience requires taking action or participating in activities that have the following two features: 1) objective value, and 2) subjective enjoyment.

Objective value means that an action or activity serves a purpose beyond the satisfaction of the person doing it. Other people would look at the action and see it as somehow helpful or useful or valuable, whether it was you doing it, or someone else. This is why people often describe something they feel as meaningful as being connecting to something "bigger than myself" or "beyond myself." For example, volunteering in a soup kitchen to feed the hungry has objective value; binge-watching "Keeping Up with the Kardashians" does not. (Note: I'm not judging your Kardashian Krush. People have the right to relax in whatever non-violent way they choose; I'm only inviting you to consider whether you would describe that time spent as "meaningful.")

Subjective enjoyment is a bit simpler: Are you having fun? Does the action or activity bring you joy or satisfaction? This is important: Working in a soup kitchen may be objectively valuable, but if you don't like doing it — you're stressed out around sharp kitchen knives and boiling soup, or you don't get along with the other volunteers, and you leave feeling drained rather than energized — you would hardly describe that experience as personally meaningful. On the flipside, wasting an afternoon playing Candy Crush on your smartphone may give you joy, but I doubt you'd consider that time meaningful. On the other hand, if there were some sort of marathon Candy Crush tournament, the proceeds of which went to fund buying cell phones for women in shelters fleeing domestic abuse, you might see that as a meaningful way to spend an afternoon.

See? A meaningful experience equals objective value plus subjective enjoyment: Service with a smile.

And a life with enough of these meaningful experiences strung together is something you will look back on as a meaningful life.

And when you look back on a meaningful life, from the vantage point of wherever you are in it — whether near the beginning, middle, or end — you don't have to ask what your purpose is; you're already living it.

You may ask: That's fine, John, but exactly *what* do I do?

This is where the Gift of Outer Work comes in: It gives us specific guidance on activities that are objectively valuable, that help people and help heal the world, including but not limited to:

- Helping the needy
- Doing acts of kindness
- Enabling others' learning
- Building community
- Being a good steward of the environment
- Working for justice

These categories of activity have two things in common. First, they are all discussed at length in ancient Jewish sacred texts. Second, all of them have real-world applications today with no shortage of challenges to be met and plenty of problems yet to solve.

Kind of makes you wonder . . . we've been working on all these areas for thousands of years, and there's still plenty of meaningful work yet to do! I admit, looking at this list may be overwhelming, and showing you the variety and breadth of all the different objectively valuable activities you can engage in may not exactly help narrow down the list.

This is where you come in. You already have within you the intuition and the insight needed to help you choose your own best Outer Work. All you have to do is answer the following questions:

- What are you good at?
- What do you enjoy doing?
- What settings do you like doing your work in?

These are the three main questions asked in the book *What Color Is Your Parachute?* by Richard Bolles, a guide to choosing and attaining your ideal career. Only instead of choosing your career, you're finding your calling, a suitable purpose to pursue in your quest for a more meaningful life.

Take some time right now to answer these questions. Take out a sheet of paper and make three lists:

1. What you're good at.

2. What you enjoy doing.

3. What setting you like working in.

Now that you have your lists, run through each of the six categories of Outer Work above, and look at the category through the lens of your three lists. Is there something in this category that I'm good at? Something I enjoy doing? Something that lets me to work in a setting I enjoy?

A lot of people respect Mother Teresa because of the selfless way she lived her life, and no one would question from the outside that her life was meaningful, but do you know anyone who would trade places with her?

If I can make a suggestion: Unless you've done volunteer work in some or all of these areas in the past,

I suggest you do a little experiment. Over the next six weeks (or months, or years, whatever it takes) schedule some time to try a volunteer activity in each of these six areas to see what it's like. Write down beforehand (in a journal, in a letter) what you expect it to be like, then afterward, write down what the experience actually was like and how it differed from your prior expectations. Did you enjoy the experience? Did you meet any nice people you'd like to see again? Did you feel competent, or like you would enjoy becoming competent in the work you were doing? Was the setting a place you would enjoy returning to?

Once the experiment is over, schedule time to return to the activities where the experience felt meaningful, and make it a regular part of your life.

Bolles added to his book an extra chapter for people of faith. It addresses the idea that many people wonder during their quest to find the right career, "What does God want me to do right now? What's God's purpose for my life?" One might think that picking a career — whether for bread and butter or as a volunteer — based on personal preferences alone is selfish, and therefore not intrinsically meaningful. Bolles, who was a pastor before he became an author, challenges this idea: If you believe in a God that might have a purpose for your life, can that God be trusted to also leave us signs for what your purpose might be? Do you believe that the same God had some hand in creating you, and fashioning you in a certain way that you have particular talents or gifts, or perhaps imbued in you your unique inclinations about the types of activities you enjoy or settings where you thrive?

If so, is it possible that these gifts and inclinations are those very signs you've been looking for?

By the way, this is how I became a rabbi, but more on that later.

Where It Comes From

When it comes to the Outer Work of repairing brokenness in the world, the Jewish tradition offers three main categories of ways to help: *tzedek* (justice through action), *tzedakah* (justice through charity), and *gemilut hasadim* (acts of kindness).

One of the most powerful verses in the Torah, in terms of the influence we are capable of having in the world (and even expected to have on the world) is *"Tzedek tzedek tirdof!"* — "Justice, justice shall you pursue!" (Deuteronomy 16:20) This reflects a core theme that runs through the whole of our sacred literature. From the very beginning, when Adam and Eve take the first bite of the apple and suddenly learn the difference between good and evil, right and wrong, we are given free will, and with it the responsibility to do what is right and what is good in the eyes of God. This reflects the micro-level pursuit of justice: Individual responsibility. This plays out again on a macro level in the Book of Exodus: The people of Israel are enslaved in Egypt, God is reminded of God's covenant with their ancestors, and God sets them free with the help of Moses and several frogs. The people leave Egypt and start wandering through the wilderness, where they complain about the lack of food and water and direction, and they yearn for the structure and security of slavery. So the question is raised: Given that we have freedom of will (we ate the apple) and freedom of action (we're not slaves), now that we *can* do anything in the world, what *should* we do? God answers this question by rallying the people around Mount Sinai and giving them the Torah, first starting with the Ten Commandments, and then the rest of it: A guide to proper living, fit for a free people. One of the key principles of a society fit for a free and holy people: Justice, justice shall you pursue!

This theme is reflected in other key verses as well. I've mentioned my favorite: Don't oppress strangers; you know what that's like, because you've been there! (Exodus 23:9) Another: Do not stand idly by the blood of your neighbor. (Leviticus 19:16) This means that we are not only to refrain from doing wrong ourselves, but that we should also actively work against wrong being done by others.

This theme also plays out in the books of the Prophets. Many people look at the words "prophet" and "prophecy", and in their minds, they associate this with a kind of future-seeing or fortune-telling, as in "a prophecy has foretold . . ." The 20th century theologian and scholar Rabbi Abraham Joshua Heschel pointed out that the primary work of many of the Prophets in the Tanakh wasn't fortune-telling; it was truth-telling, specifically, speaking truth to power. Their primary work was calling out injustice they saw in the world. Rather than being mystics or seers, they were primarily social critics who judged people who were punctilious in their religious practice and yet neglected the poor, the widow, the orphan, and other victims of the system in their day. Insofar as the Prophets spoke about the future, it was to adjure their contemporaries of the calamity that awaited them if they turned a blind eye to the injustice all around them, and later, to comfort the faithful once that calamity had finally befallen them, saying, in effect: It gets better.

How do we work for justice today? Take your pick. Ensuring that the legal system in whatever country you are in works fairly for all, ensuring it neither neglects the poor nor favors the rich. Fighting for the rights of all citizens to experience the same access to and application of justice, regardless of skin color, religious belief, or sexual identity. Ensuring that everyone to whom the rules apply play by the same rules, without unfair access to fix the game for themselves or their friends. The opportunities to pursue justice and improve the application of it abound.

You can see the same root in the Hebrew word *tzedek* — justice — and in *tzedakah*, a word commonly translated as "charity." This is because in Jewish thought, charity is less about distributing money or other help out of care or pity, and more about increasing justice in the world. See, the Torah once again has our number: While it enjoins us to work for justice, it also assumes that, as any system run by humans, our system of justice will, err, will get out of whack, and the benefits of living in a society will be unevenly and sometimes unfairly distributed. We are therefore obligated to do our part to make sure no one gets left permanently and irretrievably behind. Speaking in its time to a largely agrarian population, the Torah instructs us to leave the corners of our fields unharvested, and to not be so careful about picking up every last sheaf of grain at harvest time, so that the needy could earn their way by gleaning the leftovers in farmers' fields. (Leviticus 23:22) As the population gradually shifted to cities and commerce gained share from agriculture, this became an adjuration to be strict in using fair weights and measures, to be honest in our business dealings, and to contribute to communal collections of charity, as well as making private donations to help individuals. Specifically, we are asked to help needy brides, for whom the lack of a dowry might prevent marriage, and to see to the burial of the dead with dignity, even if their families couldn't afford a proper funeral, or they had no families to bury them.

Tzedakah also extends beyond hand-outs; we can also extend a hand up. According to Maimonides, the highest form of charity one can give is to help someone learn a trade or find a job, or lend them money to start a business.

Finally, Outer Work requires more than righting wrongs and correcting imbalances. In some ways this is just breaking even, but can we do more? Outer Work calls us to perform *gemilut hasadim* — acts of kindness. This is where we come out ahead. As I cited in the quote that began this chapter, *tzedakah* (charity) is good, but it is limited in ways *gemilut hasadim* are not. Charity can only help the poor who are also among the living; kindness can be shown to the rich and the poor alike, and to both the living and the dead. (*Sukkah* 49b)

Where I Am

To return to the idea of making Outer Work my life's work, consider Bolles: What am I good at, what do I like to do, and where do I enjoy doing it? I thought about what I like doing: learning and writing, bringing people together for fun and powerful shared experiences. I thought about what I'm good at: teaching, public speaking, getting people excited about ideas. I thought about where I like to spend my time the most: Synagogues and gatherings in my home and other people's homes. Then one day I realized that my rabbi's job included all of those things! I made an appointment with him and asked him, "How do you like your job?" He smiled and said, "I've been waiting for you to ask me that," and he handed me some pamphlets for a few rabbinical schools. The rest is history.

To be crystal clear: I'm not saying you have to be a rabbi to do your own Outer Work, or otherwise uproot your current career, go back to school to learn a whole new trade, and dedicate your life to service exclusively. But you can; you have the power to do so. You can also spend just a few hours every week, or even every month, or even every year to serving a cause greater than yourself, and if you do, I believe you will look back on a life that you have experienced as profoundly more meaningful.

What to Do

1. What's wrong with the world? (Another list!)

This exercise may get you a little tense, so be prepared. You may want to do this with the help of a relaxing beverage or some calming music. I want you to make a list of what you think is broken in the world today. Think one-line bullet points, not essays: Keep your headlines short, but you can list as many things as you like. These things can be environmental, economic, spiritual, political, nutritional . . . Anything in the world you think is a problem, as long as you really believe it's a problem, with one caveat: It can be a problem you experience personally (all the better, in fact), but it can't be only a problem for *you* alone. Next, as we've done in other exercises, score every problem on your list by how passionate you are about seeing this problem solved, how inspired you personally feel to act, on a scale of 1 ("Meh.") to 10 ("Let's get this done *yesterday*, people!"). Once again, try scoring everything without using the number 7; force yourself to round down to 6 or up to 8, to eliminate mediocre non-evaluation. Finally, pick your top three things with scores of at least 8 or above, and move on to the next exercise . . .

2. Educate yourself on the issues you're most passionate about.

It's time to get up to speed and equip yourself to heal the world. Take a look at the three issues you identified, and for each one, ask yourself, "Am I an expert on this?" You may very well be, especially if you're passionate about it, but if you're not an expert yet, you can become versant in the subject in no time, or at least knowledgeable enough to be helpful. If you're a book reader (what am I saying?!), find the best two books on each of your three areas. How do you find the best books? You can search Amazon using your own description of the issue, and it may show you books that rank highly rated for that subject. Better yet, if you have a friend who is also passionate about your subject, ask them which two books they would recommend for someone just learning about this issue. Now you have six books on three different subjects you're passionate about. Read all of them, or at least skim. If you're not a book person, find some other ways to educate yourself: watch documentaries or YouTube videos, listen to podcasts or read activists' blogs, or best of all, talk to people who volunteer in the fields that interest you. Once you're up to speed on your three issues, pick one problem to solve — just one for now! — and move on to the next exercise.

3. Identify groups that address this issue.

Now that you've got a problem to solve that you are passionate *and* educated about, it's time to identify people and groups to work with. For any problem in the world worth solving — and if you're passionate about it, it is — no one can, should, or needs to solve it alone.

Not to say that there's never a time when a leader needs to stand alone to inspire others, and someday, you may need to be that very leader, but first you should try to find other leaders to follow and other followers to connect with (this Gift tends to double for Community!). If the problem has a local manifestation, use the internet to find all the groups in your area who might work on this issue locally. If it's on a grander scale, but there is no way to help in your own town with your own hands, look for ways to help from afar through groups that are closer to the action. This is still in the category of doing your homework. Do an internet search about the groups you identify; see what press there is about them — good or bad — and make sure you identify one or more groups that you trust. Then, when you have your cause, when you've learned what you can from afar, and when you've found a person or group to connect with, tackle the next exercise.

4. Volunteer with this group.

This is beginning to feel like one long exercise, right? You're not wrong. Make a plan (preferably with a friend) to volunteer with a person or group that is working for the cause of your choosing. Call or email them, find out when a thing to do is, and schedule your commitment to help out. Try writing down your expectations — how you think the experience will be, what you hope to get out of it. Then, prepare yourself to enter the experience with an open mind, and be prepared to help out however they tell you that you are needed most. In my experience with volunteering in new places, it's almost never exactly how I expect it will be. I've passionately planned to feed the hungry, and then I've arrived and learned about hairnets and gloves and food service work, all the gritty details that you have to get right to fulfill the higher mission. Be respectful to the leaders on-site; they are usually way more experienced than you, perhaps having been committed to the cause for years, and are often themselves volunteers. No matter how successful or important you are in your day-to-day career, when you first volunteer for a cause, be prepared to start at the bottom. If you stick with it, you may find that your unique talents as a management consultant or a pastry chef may have the opportunity to shine through and help the cause. But if you're just starting out, grab a hairnet, newbie!

5. Try your hand at fundraising.

While you can begin to repair the world by simple acts of kindness and adding your holy spark in ways large and small, every organized effort to repair the world on a grander scale takes money, and lots of it. Even all-volunteer organizations have costs for office supplies, web hosting, art supplies for protest signs, donuts for volunteers, you name it, and someone who has experience and skill in bringing in money can be a real asset to any cause. Ask your group how they do fundraising and how you can help. Some have phone-bank days where a number of people get together and call others on a prepared list or simply call their friend and make a pitch to support the cause. Some do special events like bake sales, garage sales, or even sporting events. I've run two marathons for a charity that helps seriously ill children go to a special summer camp that's equipped with extra medical facilities. At any organized 5k, 10k, half- or full-marathon you'll see people wearing swag from different charities because they are running to raise money and awareness about their cause. Most people are shy about fundraising — that's why it's such a valuable skill — because they think it feels like begging, but the most important thing to remember is this: You're not asking for yourself; you're asking for a cause you believe in, and if you find someone else who believes in it, too, you're doing them a favor by connecting them with an opportunity to help. You're not selling yourself; you're really selling the opportunity for people to connect to a cause greater than themselves — finding their own meaning by living their own purpose — which is exactly what you're there for, too. If you help them do that, they will not only be generous toward your cause; they will grateful to you for helping them.

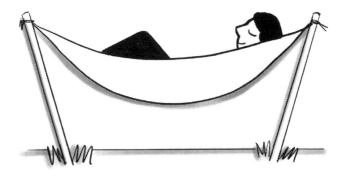

THE SEVENTH GIFT
REST

"More than the Jews have kept the Sabbath, the Sabbath has kept the Jews."

— Ahad Ha'am

"The trouble with the rat race is that even if you win, you're still a rat."

— Lily Tomlin

Any musician will tell you: sometimes the most important notes are the "rests" — the beats of silence between the notes they play. This Gift of Rest encourages you to develop a habit of pausing and unplugging regularly and intentionally, to appreciate the world as it is — and ourselves as we are — ignoring the impulse to create or fix. This fosters a sense of sufficiency, critical to feeling the abundance in our lives, and it also allows us to refresh and recharge to continue the work of growth.

Where You Are

You are toast.

You are crumbling, black, carbon-smelling burnt toast.

From the moment you wake up (or from the moment your better nature overcomes the snooze bar) you are at a dead sprint. Getting yourself ready for the day, getting the kids up and ready and out the door to school, and getting yourself to the office or jobsite . . . this is just the opening act. You grind through the day with more meetings than time, you pack up what you couldn't get done because you had meetings, endure your commute — because no matter how early you got in to beat the traffic, most people are tapped out around the same time, so the evening rush is worse — at home in time for dinner (maybe), reliving your grade-school nightmare of homework with the kids, doing their bedtime ritual, and then getting to your homework, instead of spending quality time with your significant other, who may have homework of his or her own, or you dodge your work to put on some television, in front of which you pass out from exhaustion, punting your overflowing skiff of work until the next day. Maybe there will be fewer meetings! Right? And then, before you know it . . . Snooze bar. Rinse. Repeat.

But there's always the weekend.

Right?

But that's when the skiff of work bumps against the dock of your one safe harbor, the day or two when they're not allowed to schedule meetings.

Right?

Let's stipulate that there are no meetings on the weekend, no days when you have to go into work to catch up. What were you doing all day, anyway? Let's further stipulate that you don't have to go to a second job, or a third, or your side-hustle driving Uber or delivering pizza just to make ends meet. If all this is true, then at last! You get to do all the cleaning and shopping and laundry and cooking and bill-paying and car-washing and lawn-painting and yak-shaving you couldn't get to during the week, because you were at your job, shaving someone else's yak. Unless, of course, you are an entrepreneur or otherwise self-employed, in which case, of course you are working on the weekend, because the reality is, that being your own boss means you have the most hard-charging boss, the one who's already heard all of your excuses, because your own boss made them.

And forget about seeing your spouse or significant other, because they are likely in the same grind as you. If you're smart and disciplined, you have a regular date-night scheduled during which I'm sure you never check your smartphone, never answer a ping or a text or a call from a boss or a client or a co-worker or an employee or a yak.

Right?

Forget about the kids. They are already overscheduled with sports and birthday parties and social engagements and tutoring and homework and maybe chores (if you're not doing them all this weekend). If you're lucky to be able to, you'll feel great about making it to practices and games, lessons and recitals, but you are not so lucky and so able that you are not checking your phone the entire time, hoping that they notice you are present, but also hoping that they don't notice that you are not actually present. You are looking at your phone.

But . . . You're important. Right?

Pop quiz: If you're so important, why are you killing yourself?

If we need you so much, why are you working yourself to death, so we won't have you anymore?

If you're so important, why do you have to answer every ping or text or call, to jump at every ball, asking the question, "How high?"

Of course, you are needed. You are wanted. We all like to feel needed and wanted. But does the extent to which other people seem to own your time, make you feel like you matter, really matter to them on a personal level, or are you just being a victim of I-It, just because you need money? And usually, it's the people you care least about who take most advantage of this, while the people you care about the most seem have lost their time-privileges with you.

Even if you are totally self-directed, totally in control of your own time, even if you have wisely allocated a little of that time toward some things as frivolous as rest and relaxation, you're probably still taking calls from work. Worst part: you may be trusting a little too much that those who love you the most will understand that you are not around, and why.

Smell that?

I think you burnt your toast.

Where You Are Going

What would it mean to you to be totally at peace: Satisfied with the world as it is, satisfied with yourself and your accomplishments, satisfied with the relationships you already have, the stuff you've already accumulated, the work you've already done? What would it mean to you to have the sense of power and freedom necessary to put your smartphone in a drawer for 24 hours and not check it?

Imagine saying to yourself: "My boss can wait to hear from me until tomorrow."

Imagine saying to yourself: "Whatever happens in the world outside my home and my immediate family, I can deal with it later, and that will be fine."

Imagine saying to yourself: "I know amazing and cute cat videos are appearing on Facebook right this instant, but the very best ones will still be online tomorrow for me to LOL." What if, instead, you LOLed at a joke someone told you in person? What if you engaged in a heated debate about politics with a human being in the same room (which, as it turns out, is much less likely to get you "unfriended")? What if you spent a full day engaging in real interpersonal relationships that would sustain you throughout the week, regardless of any problems that might have come up by unplugging?

So many of us feel overtired, overworked, overtaxed, and running on empty. What would it mean to your health and stress level if you took one day a week *off*, and then returned refreshed and recharged?

You might say: "But I'm too important. People need me! If I unplug, I'm letting people down. And if I let people down at my job, I'm not taking proper care of my family."

I agree with you: You *are* important. You are too important to let people down by cracking under the pressure and getting sidelined by the exhaustion — not to mention the health problems and lack of focus that comes with it — of the 24/7 hustle. What's the worst thing that could happen if you settled for 24/6?

Put another way, what's the *best* thing that could happen if you took a 52-day vacation every year, and paced it out one day a week to reap the ongoing benefits?

You can return to the struggle and the hustle at the top of your game, at least partially — if not fully — refreshed, with renewed energy and focus. And don't be fooled: Rest time isn't wasted time. It is instead a perfect opportunity to invest time and attention in the most important relationships in your life — your spouse or significant other, your family, your closest friends — and invest time and attention in really knowing and appreciating yourself. So in addition to having greater energy and focus, your renewed self-awareness and the stronger bonds of your most important relationships will support you to achieve and grow in ways you could never accomplish sustainably by giving in to the 24/7 grind.

It all starts with this basic principle: You are enough, the world is sufficient as-is, and you are ultimately free to do whatever you wish.

This is important, so I'm going to repeat it:

You are enough.

The world is sufficient as it is.

You are ultimately free to do whatever you wish.

If you've read the whole book up to this point, this principle may seem counterintuitive and perhaps even contradictory to the other ideas in this book. Why would a book dedicated to positive change and personal growth — with specific steps to take to accomplish that — tell me I'm fine just the way I am?

Why would a book that challenges me to heal the world — again with the specific steps! — tell me the world is just fine as-is?

And why on earth would a book that talks about the Gifts that lead us to a life of better choices tell me I can do whatever I wish?!

I thought of putting this practice first, because I fully believe that loving yourself as you are and loving the world as it is can be the healthiest foundation for growth. Nevertheless, I realize that many people begin this journey, as I did, with a sense of brokenness, with a sense of having a piece missing, and that's what prompts you to seek a path or a method or a technology for a better life. That's probably what prompted you to find this book and read this far. You've done so much work to get here! And that's awesome. I'm proud of you. Here's the reward: You get to rest.

You don't get to stop, but you do get to rest.

When I say you are fine as you are, I mean you already have all the tools, materials, and strength you need to start to grow. Or don't start, and you're still OK in my book. You are already worthy of love and sustenance. So take one day a week to pause, acknowledge that and revel in it, before you continue on your path.

When I say the world is fine as it is, I mean that it is strong enough to keep turning for one day without your pushing it, so take a break from trying to fix it, realize how good it already is, even if it could be better. Everything that needs healing will still need healing tomorrow; meanwhile, feel free to enjoy the blessings you already have while you appreciate the progress you have already made in healing the world.

When I say you are free to do whatever you wish, I mean it. Receiving a Gift does not bind your free will as to whether you will open it, use it, enjoy it, return it, or cast it aside. All the Gifts in this book presume free will. The Gift of Rest is special, though: This Gift is itself in celebration of your freedom of will and your capacity to set aside the world's demands on your sweat and your creativity. It is a freedom *from*, in addition to a freedom *to*. In the words of the open-source software community, the Gift of Rest is not only "free, as in speech," but also "free, as in beer."

Where It Comes From

I also decided to put this Gift in the seventh place because of its association with the number seven, which represents both completion and wholeness in the Jewish tradition, just as the world took a full cycle of seven days to complete (including the creation of Rest). If the Gift of Learning is the fire-starter and fuel for all the other Gifts, then the Gift of Rest is the S'mores. I saved the best for last.

Perhaps the most powerful, persistent, and pervasive technology that the Jewish people have given the world is *Shabbat*. The Hebrew word *Shabbat* means to pause or cease; it's where the English words "sabbath" and "sabbatical" come from. It first occurs in our sacred literature as the grand finale to our creation story: God spent six days creating the world, and seeing that everything created was good in and of itself and sufficient for people's needs, God rested on the seventh day.

> "The heavens and the earth were finished, and all their array. On the seventh day God finished the work that God had been doing, and God ceased on the seventh day from all the work that God had done. And God blessed the seventh day and declared it holy, because on it God ceased from all the work of creation that God had done."
>
> (Genesis 2:1-3)

If we can see God's behavior as a model for our behavior when exercising our capacity for wisdom, judgment, and creativity, why would we stop short of imitating God's capacity for Rest?

The next time we see this in the text is in the revelation of the Torah to the Hebrews and their fellow travelers after being freed from slavery in Egypt. This newly-free people walk through the wilderness for about seven weeks (there's that number again!) and then find themselves at the foot of a mountain, Mount Sinai. Moses tells them to wait there and get ready for an important message. Three days later, God speaks the Ten Commandments to all the people present, the fourth of which is:

> "Remember the Sabbath day and keep it holy. Six days shall you labor and do all your work, but the seventh day is a Sabbath day of the Lord your God: You shall not do any work — you, your son or daughter, your male or female workers, your cattle, or the stranger who is within your settlements. For in six days the Lord made heaven and earth and sea, and all that is in them, and God rested on the seventh day; therefore the Lord blessed the Sabbath day and hallowed it."
>
> (Exodus 20:8-11)

Ever since then, this concept of a whole day of rest every week, first connected to creation, has also been linked with our exodus from Egypt — more importantly, our exodus from slavery. In simpler terms: One of the hallmarks of a free people is the ability to take a day off.

Today, different people observe this day of rest differently. Jews do it on Saturday; most Christians do it on Sunday. The standard American work week is Monday through Friday, which accommodates both. Among Jews you see a wide variety of practices associated with this day: Some may take it as a day to drive up the coast to their favorite restaurant. Some go to the movies or a museum. Some avoid all creative activity, to imitate God on the seventh day of creation, but some find the best way to relax is to dig in the garden or paint a picture. Some don't drive, cook, use any electronic devices, or spend any money all day, but they still spend a packed day enjoying big family meals (prepared or purchased ahead of time, to prevent working or transacting business during Shabbat), and perhaps time with community at the synagogue for prayer and Torah study, then balance it out with some hardcore napping. This last way is my favorite, but you do you.

Where I Am

As I began to advance in my first career as a financial analyst, the corporate world expected greater and greater access to my attention to meet deadlines and get deals done. The 40-hour week quickly grew into 24/7 always-on-call expectations. I didn't (usually) go into the office on the weekends, but the office was always buzzing away in my pocket or pinging away on my laptop, and there were consequences for not jumping for the ball at the whistle. This kept the stress of the office as a constant dull hum just at the periphery of my awareness, and it interfered with my ability to relax and to really enjoy time with my family when I (and they) knew I could have to jump at any moment. To be clear: I was never a heart surgeon, or an FBI agent, or a volunteer fireman, or a nuclear reactor meltdown specialist. I was a financial analyst who worked in a regular cubicle farm of a company, and yet it seemed I had all the on-call demand and stress of a drug dealer.

And when there was time away from the office, it was all I could do to keep up with the business of life: cutting the grass, washing the dog, shaving the yak; shopping for groceries, work clothes, and yak-shaving supplies; paying the bills and balancing the books; paying perfunctory attention to my kids' homework assignments and sports practices; dulling the anxiety during the gaps in activity by immersive television-watching.

The benefits for me in observing a day of rest have been enormous. First off, I hate shopping malls — the crowds, the crass consumerism, but mostly the parking. When I started observing Shabbat, and someone in my family wanted to go to the mall, I was like, "No can do!" Phew. Most importantly, though, it's become a regular appointment with re-immersion in family life. For the most part, my wife, my kids, and I are apart for most of our waking hours, between our work and their school. And sure, the weeknight evenings are still a hustle of chores and maintenance and dinners of microwaved leftovers between the long workdays and occasional sleep. But Shabbat is a time when we put our screens away, eat more leisurely family meals together, have friends over, play board games, Barbies, Legos, and again with the hardcore napping.

Of course, as a rabbi in a synagogue community, I lead religious services and teach Torah on Shabbat. People often ask how I can tell others to take off their jobs for Shabbat when I am visibly doing mine? But (don't tell my congregation this) I would do these things even if I wasn't getting paid to, and any Jew who's knowledgeable can lead services or teach Torah, rabbi or not. And people in my community know that I won't answer my phone, email, or texts on Shabbat, and they don't ask for any other work from me, because that's the expectation I set. So, aside from a couple of hours in the "office" (synagogue sanctuary) and another hour of lunch and conversation with my congregants (more like a lunch break and a social experience for me with my friends than it is like work), Shabbat is like a mini-vacation or staycation that I look forward to every week, and that

I've come to count on to decompress from the week before and recharge for the coming week.

The traditional Jewish way of observing a day of peace is pretty intricate and takes practice. (We're so conditioned to hustle 24/7 that we have to be retrained to be still!) If the practice of unplugging and black-belt-level chillaxation is new for you, I suggest trying the following exercises, one at a time, then adding them together as you go, over a period of a few weeks.

What to Do

1. Host a "Friday Night Friends" dinner party.

This can be a formal affair, if that's your thing, but if that's too daunting for you, then I suggest starting with as low a bar as you need to in order to make it happen: Casual, come-as-you-are, everyone bring something. The point is to get people together, in your home, with no other agenda than to relax, eat, and enjoy each other's company. At some point, go around the table and ask each person to share something good that happened during the week, something they're grateful for, or something they like about the people sitting next to them. Make this dinner a "no phone zone" — provide a drawer or basket to hold people's phones during dinner. Have wine, or don't. Play board games after. Follow up with your guests afterwards, thank them for coming, and if others found it to be a positive experience, suggest one of your friends host the next one soon.

2. Set the Rest Expectation.

If you're someone people expect to be able to reach 24/7, start retraining them to expect 24/6. Designate a period of 24 consecutive hours sometime in your week (mine is sundown Friday to sundown Saturday) to go "off the grid" . . . no cabin in the woods necessary, just don't answer phone calls, texts, emails, Tweets, or trolling comments on your Facebook posts. See what happens! Most likely any message can wait 24 hours before being answered, and any disasters that occur will be recoverable. Consider setting an out-of-office message on your email, if necessary. Revise as needed if you are in fact an on-call emergency first responder or awaiting an organ transplant; there's a long-standing exception to the commandment to Rest, and that is taking any action necessary to save a life. Otherwise, the world can wait. If you'd like to validate this with real data, after the Rest period, write down all the messages you got (via phone, email, text, etc.) during the Rest period. Then, put a star next to all of them that really could not have waited: You missed a business or work opportunity, something critical that depended on you failed, someone was disappointed in you in a way that has long-term consequences for your relationship. My guess? Very few stars, or none at all. If you have a lot of stars, ask yourself: Do I want to live a life where I can't peace-out for 24 hours without someone else making me feel like a failure?

3. Start your To-Don't List.

Whatever your day of rest is, challenge yourself to pick one normal life-maintenance chore (grocery shopping, balancing your check book, sorting your recycling, shampooing your hamster) and plan to give yourself the day off from that activity. You can get extra groceries the day before, and your hamster can be unkempt for one more day. The following week, keep that one chore on the To-Don't List, and add one more (cutting the grass, doing the laundry, buying hamster chow). Repeat each week until you achieve a whole day of total rest, not doing anything you wouldn't choose to do if you didn't have to, like you're in a luxury suite in a tropical getaway somewhere. If you imagine yourself in a happy place like this, removed from worries and chores, and then you think of your usual To-Do List, and you see yourself saying, "That can wait until I get back," then it belongs on the To-Don't List. The point of this exercise is to see that it is not only paid-employment tasks that can exhaust us, but also the chores of maintaining our personal comfort and security that can be set aside for one full day of Rest, much to our benefit.

4. Take advantage of your freedom.

Fill the day you've emptied by enjoying a book you've been meaning to get to, spending time with a local friend you never see, or getting reacquainted with your partner or children, whom your usual hustle may have turned into strangers. Board games help, as does wine, if that's your thing. (Maybe not with the children.) Rest does not mean arbitrarily enforced boredom; it is an opportunity to relax and refresh and reconnect with the people who matter to you most, and to spend unrushed, uninterrupted time with yourself. It is an opportunity to appreciate and express gratitude for the world as it is, for people as they are, including yourself as you are, without scratching the itch to improve anything or anyone, especially yourself. The paradox is that through Rest you will improve, as will the quality of the relationships in your life, as well as the quality of the work you return to, once you are rested and refreshed — not because you did anything about it, but specifically because you avoided doing anything about it. Funny how that works, but it does.

5. Join a Rest Community.

You can spend the day alone, if that's your peace, but it's preferable to spend at least part of it with people. A synagogue, a church, a kickball game, or an AA meeting are all places where the main purpose is to gather people with similar interests and values to support each other. Seek social places (where you don't have to buy something) to be with other people. Spiritual activities are popular for this, like religious services, in part because the regular observance of a weekly day of Rest is an integral part of many religions' traditions, but also because honoring the spiritual aspect of our lives is something that we can make room for when we set aside the busy-ness of making a living and avoid filling the gap with mundane chores. This Rest Community could be the place you found "Shul Shopping" in the chapter on the Gift of Community, or it could be a group of friends you organize specifically for the purpose of getting together and kicking back on a weekly basis. To see the value of this Rest community, maybe spend one Rest day alone, then one Rest day with the community, and see the difference community makes in your experience of Rest. I'm willing to bet that community, as usual, makes a good thing better.

CONCLUSION
THE PATH

"If you are not a better person tomorrow than you are today, what need have you for a tomorrow?"
— Rebbe Nachman of Breslov

"I find the great thing in this world is not so much where we stand, as in what direction we are moving: To reach the port of heaven, we must sail sometimes with the wind and sometimes against it — but we must sail, and not drift, nor lie at anchor."
— Oliver Wendell Holmes Sr.

This chapter concludes our journey together by describing for you the road ahead: How to approach the path before you, what first steps to take, the next steps after that, and if you're interested, a big step that is not required to get something out of this book, but that you may have already considered or are now considering:

joining the Jewish people. We finish by reviewing the three promises I made to you in the beginning of the book, and if I kept those promises, I have one thing to ask of you in return.

How to Proceed

I said this in the beginning, but now that you've learned about the Seven Gifts along this path and may be excited to get started, it's worth reiterating: Start slow. Even though you may be ready for growth and hungry to see all the changes in your life this path promises immediately, avoid the temptation to try to master everything at once. If you jump in the deep end before testing the waters and acclimating deliberately, you may find yourself overwhelmed, and instead of immediate and profound change, you are more likely to experience immediate culture shock, and you are more likely to quit before you experience deep, lasting results. I do not want this to happen to you. Not that it's a competition, but it's worth contemplating the adage: Slow and steady wins the race.

Another take on this old saw from Aesop's fable about the tortoise and the hare comes from a training mantra of the Navy Seals: Slow is smooth, and smooth is fast. When a Seal is training a new skill or tactic, he may deliberately slow down at first, to make sure he can fully and effectively complete all of the intermediate steps on his way to completion. By slowing down, his operation becomes smoother, more natural, and more fluid, with each iteration of the process. As his actions become more fluid, he naturally gets faster with each repetition of the skill or tactic. Start slow, because slowness and deliberateness engender smoothness, and what we learn to do smoothly, we begin to do faster.

Perhaps a better example is that of a musician learning a new piece of music, one that is complicated and has many different movements or distinct sections. Unless the musician is a savant that can sight-read a piece and play the entire thing perfectly the first time through, or one who already has years and years of experience with similar pieces, that musician is probably going to begin learning the piece by learning and practicing one movement at a time, gaining some basic level of competence and confidence with each section before moving onto the next section.

This is like that. Unless you are a spiritual savant — some are, I guess, but most of us are not — or you already have years and years of experience with a similar set of spiritual disciplines, I believe that attempting to master all of these practices quickly and simultaneously is more likely to be counterproductive, and you are more likely to become overwhelmed and give up before you experience any real or lasting growth.

I recommend instead working on one practice at a time, either in the order in which they appear in this book (which I chose deliberately), or in the order in which they most appeal to you. There's something to be said for starting with that which feels most natural and easiest to assimilate, and then take on the next-easiest, and so on, finishing with that which seems most foreign or difficult. By then you will have gained the confidence and the sense of competence in your practice to the point where, suddenly, that which seemed most challenging to you from the outset now seems so easy, you might wonder why you put it off.

Slow is smooth, and smooth is fast.

One more recommendation: As you take on these practices slowly, I suggest you also do them cumulatively; that is, once you've begun to master the first one, or at least feel like you're beginning to get the hang of it, continue to practice it while you take on a new practice — as a background process, if you will. While it may seem overwhelming to imagine doing all of these things every day — and really, you probably won't be doing all of them every day, even once you've mastered them, but on average you'll touch on all of them every week or every month — there are millions of people in the Jewish world who undertake all of these practices simultaneously and habitually, whether they started learning as small children, or as a 40-year-old shepherd. That said, please don't judge yourself if you don't reach this level of proficiency any time soon. Just know, by their example, that it is possible.

First Steps

There's a teaching in *Pirkei Avot,* a collection of the wisdom of our Sages from about 2,000 years ago, on the best way to go about a journey of learning and growth.

> "Get yourself a teacher.
> Find yourself a friend.
> Judge everyone favorably."
>
> (*Pirkei Avot* 1:6)

You may recognize elements of this passage from exercise in the Gift of Learning; here I'm giving you the complete source, including one more step. Let's break these down:

Get yourself a teacher.

To be successful on your path, it's important that you have a guide along your way. If you're pursuing the practices that are in this book, I recommend that you find a local rabbi, preferably one who can make the time to meet with you on a regular basis, to discuss with her or him what you are learning. Following the steps in this book is a start, but to get the most out of it, you will need someone in as a guide who not only is familiar with the Gifts, but also one who is able to get to know you and can help you grow by focusing your attention on the learning that will benefit you as a unique individual.

If you need help finding a rabbi in your area, connect with me through the Promised Life Tribe, and I will reach out to my network and do my best to help you find a teacher close to you. However, I understand that not everyone lives in a community with access to rabbis, or what rabbis you can find may not be able to meet with you regularly. If that is the case for you, I encourage you to let me know through the Tribe, and I will be happy to be your guide for this stage of your journey.

Find yourself a friend.

One thing about learning that our Sages figured out long ago is that while having a teacher is important, just as important is having a peer to learn with. Typically, a rabbi has a number of students, and rather than just lecturing the students about the meaning of a text, the rabbi gives the students something to learn together, to wrestle with themselves, to share ideas with each other, debate meaning, and add to one another's understanding by multiplying perspectives. Only after the students have worked together does the teacher test their understanding and fill in the gaps. This kind of peer mentoring not only helps you see what you're learning from a different angle; it also fosters friendships gives social support to your journey, thereby making it easier to stick to the path and enhance your chance for success.

My advice here is to share this book with someone you know who might benefit from it, and if you both agree to give it a try, make a plan to learn and practice the steps together. If you can't find someone right away locally, and you want to connect with others who are working on this program already, the best thing for you to join the Promised Life Tribe for updates on communities that are forming now, both local and online, to discuss these ideas and work on these practices together.

Finally, the most successful way to have a good friend in your life who supports you on your journey is to *be* a good friend and provide that support to someone else. If you're going to ask someone to be there for you, make sure you are there for them. That's the deal, and that's how friendships work best.

Judge everyone favorably.

When beginning a journey of discovery, whether your journey is as simple as trying a new restaurant or as bold as moving to a new country, it is important to take that first step (and most steps thereafter) with an open mind. Important: This does not mean suspending our judgment altogether. A better translation of this phrase is "give others the benefit of the doubt" or better yet "slightly tip the scales of judgement in others' favor."

As the saying goes, to get results you've never gotten, you have to be willing to try something you've never tried, and this approach often challenges our assumptions, our prior learning, and the rules we have constructed for operating in our world. So first we must be gentle with ourselves and give ourselves permission to act in new ways that we didn't think we had the capacity or permission to act.

This does not mean accepting everything anyone tells you without question or weighing it against your own prior experience. In fact, I am on this path precisely because what I have learned so far in my own study and practice in Judaism is MORE consistent with and reflective of my own experience than the religion and culture I was born into and any other value system that was handed to me. You should absolutely subject any idea I share with you to your own judgment and the scrutiny of your own reason. What it does mean is being more open-minded toward the people you meet along the way.

Jewish wisdom and practice attract people from every walk of life, across any spectrum you can think of: geographic, political, racial, socio-economic, gender, sexual orientation, sports-team loyalty, what have you. As I said, I believe it can benefit everyone, everywhere . . . and that means you may find yourself pursuing this path alongside people who are very different from you, with whom dedication to these practices may be the only thing you appear to have in common. And that's OK, because all of these practices were designed (or evolved) to work in diverse communities. The *Talmud* itself is an encyclopedic collection of arguments over how to interpret the Torah and follow its precepts, 99 percent of which arguments ended in "agree to disagree." And yet it is said of the scholars who disagreed most bitterly that their children would marry one another; that takes some serious "benefit of the doubt" thinking.

I'll go one step further: This kind of thinking has become, unfortunately, countercultural. As digital networks and social media have opened us to connection with more and more diverse people and cultures, it has also allowed us to connect with more and more like-minded people, to the point where we can retreat into digital bubbles in the exclusive company of only those with whom we agree 100 percent, which has in turn led us to objectify all those who are different from us. Arguments against others (and otherness) have escalated to the point of toxicity, and the very technology which has enabled greater pluralism has also generated more divisiveness.

I'd like to propose this idea of "judge everyone favorably" as a disruptive technology that may serve as antidote to this kind of divisiveness. If we can agree on sharing these seven practices, regardless of who we are or where we come from, we can risk encounter with diverse people without having to concede other values we hold dear or subjecting others to such concession. If those with power and voice in the political or "culture-war" landscape were willing to make the same commitment, how much less toxic would the airwaves and Twitter feeds be?

Final point on this topic: When in learning mode, we also often form judgments about people by comparing ourselves to them on the dimension of learning or progress. We compare ourselves to those more learned, who've been working at it longer or have more natural aptitude for certain things, and we may judge them as arrogant or aloof, but more likely we judge ourselves as deficient and become discouraged. On the flip side, having acquired some learning or progress, we may be tempted to judge others who have not progressed in their learning as far as we have.

For example, I was tutoring a student in preparation for his becoming *bar mitzvah*, the state of Jewish legal majority that occurs when a boy reaches ages 13, often marked by a celebration in which the child participates publicly in leading services for a congregation. This young man had learned to say a certain prayer in front of the congregation that is usually said by a number of adults in a given service, and during his celebration, his mother would be saying the same prayer in public. Having just learned a prayer, to be sung in Hebrew, by rigorous practice, it happens that he sang it more fluently than his mother, who learned it many years before but also hadn't practiced it in many years. Now, in my experience every teenager knows everything, and every parent of teenagers know next to nothing; at least this was my experience as a teenager, and my recently-teenage sons would verify this. But when we were preparing for the service, the boy was giving his mother a hard time because she couldn't say the prayer as well as he could, at which point I took him aside as his rabbi.

"Did you ever read the Spiderman comic book?"

"No, but I saw the movies." Sheesh.

"What are Uncle Ben's last words to Peter Parker?"

Easy one, duh. "With great power comes great responsibility."

"It applies here, too, but I'll put a twist on it: Great learning, such as you've achieved, requires great humility. In many subjects your mother has learned more than you will ever know, though she may have forgotten or become a bit rusty in some areas. You should celebrate your learning and be proud of what you know, and you should also give your mother the benefit of the doubt. And you will learn a few things from her yet."

Although if this boy is like me, he may be in his 30s before he begins to realize how wise his parents really are.

So as you progress on this path, remember to judge the people you meet favorably, with an open heart and an open mind. This applies to your teacher, who has many things to show you that may challenge you. This applies to your friends and peers in learning, who may have a completely different take on what you are learning together. And this applies to all whom you meet along the path. Don't entirely suspend your judgment about new ideas; this is not a cult, and there is no Kool-Aid, but when it comes to your fellow travelers, be generous in judging people favorably.

Next Steps

I've said it before, and I'll say it again: The single best thing you can do to ensure that the change you create in your life is successful and enduring is to get involved with a community of people like you, people who are on the same path toward meaning, joy, and personal growth. Many hands make light work, and the best cure for a stumble is a helping hand up. There are four ways you can leverage the power of community to get the most out of the Gifts in this book: go deeper with the community you already belong to, join an online community, join a physical community, or start your own community.

First, if you already belong to a community that nurtures your growth, supports you when you struggle, and allows you to nurture and support others, *mazal tov*! You have a gift in your life that fewer and fewer people experience these days. If your community does not currently offer space and support for the practices in this book, consider introducing them to your community: talk about them, share the book, see whether a few of your friends might be willing to take on a group experiment of challenging each other to work through one or more of the chapters together. Bring up this book to a book club and see if there's interest in discussing it. See if your rabbi, pastor, shaman, gang leader, or spin instructor might be willing to teach a class on it, if you think it might be beneficial to others in your group. Chances are, if you found this book helpful, other people in your community or social circle will, too.

Second, you can join an online community of others who are reading this book around the country and around the globe and who may be working through the same chapters you are right this instant. Look for details at the back of this book on how to join the Promised Life Tribe, an online community I moderate where people just like you can connect, share their successes, and workshop their struggles around the practices in this book and the challenges they face in life. Members of the Tribe will also get updates about new-and-improved future editions of this book, as well as information about in-real-life gatherings in physical locations near you and upcoming opportunities for focused study of one or more of the Gifts in this book.

Third, if you're not already part of a community that feeds you intellectually, socially, or spiritually, join one. I refer you back to the chapter on the Fourth Gift: Community for strategies on how to find a community that's right for you. I can't speak for all organizations, but I can tell you that most synagogues I've been a part of welcome newcomers who are "shul shopping" regardless of where you are coming from; just be respectful of the community and its existing mission if you are coming from someplace totally different. Don't come with your own agenda or message to spread, but be willing to hear what they have to say before you talk too much. Take a class there, attend a service or meeting that is open to or designed for newcomers. If you feel a connection, go back again, as often as you're comfortable. If you like, you can reach out to the Promised Life Tribe for recommendations of welcoming communities near you.

Fourth, and this is a baller, black-belt move: Start your own community. Most of the practices in this book are improved when undertaken with at least one other person; if one more is good, many more can be better. If you have shared these practices with others, or another person has shared them with you, then consider organizing yourselves to get together regularly — over coffee, brunch, powerlifting, knitting, meditation, or band practice — to discuss these ideas, check in on each other's growth, or plan to deepen your learning in some related subject. Feel free to use the Promised Life Tribe to organize a meetup in your area, and then take the initiative to lead your own Tribe. Heck, the next edition of this book may be the one that you write, sharing your experience as a practitioner and as a leader who has taken responsibility for the growth, meaning, joy, and connection of others. Nothing would please me more.

A Big Step

I declared at the beginning that my goal in writing this book for you was not, and never has been, to encourage you to convert to Judaism, if you're not already Jewish. That was my path, and I came to it in my own good time, of my own volition, and that's really the only way that it can be successfully and sincerely accomplished.

Nevertheless, I recognize that some people reading this book may be on the path to conversion already; maybe you're reading it as part of your curriculum for a conversion class, or maybe you found the book in your journey to learn more about Judaism before you take the next step toward conversion. I also recognize that in my experience teaching Introduction to Judaism classes, which have a curriculum designed to give a complete preliminary understanding of Judaism for those who fully intend to convert, that many students who began the class with no such intention then encountered a tradition and a community that spoke to them and inspired them in ways they didn't expect, and over the course of their study, or perhaps soon after the conclusion of the class, they decided to "take the plunge" (you'll get this pun in a moment) — like I did many years ago, and like some of my recent students have done.

If this describes your present feeling or intention, or if you just have the inkling that you'd like to know more about what's involved before you make an important lifetime commitment to a strong, durable, but occasionally persecuted people, then this section is for you; read on.

There is an impression in contemporary culture that when you approach a rabbi about conversion to Judaism, that rabbi is supposed to turn you away three times before accepting you as a student to begin the process. This impression even made it into the popular Netflix series "Orange Is the New Black" when one of the inmates decided to convert to Judaism, perhaps initially because the kosher meals in her prison were better than the standard prison fare. But as she learns more about Judaism to answer her friends' questions about it, she finds more and more about it to be attractive as a world view and as a way to live. A rabbi comes to the prison to check the legitimacy of her claim of requiring a kosher diet, and he immediately rejects her. She asks to convert to Judaism, not just for the food, but because what she's learned besides the dietary laws has impressed her as well. He rejects her again. Then she fully opens up about why Judaism has been so personally meaningful for her. The rabbi is moved, and he says, "Ask me one more time."

This was a beautiful moment, in a show I have loved to watch. Also: That never happens. I have never seen a rabbi stick to the practice of turning someone away a fixed number of times before accepting them, nor have I practiced this myself. The Three-Times thing is an urban legend with no basis in Jewish law. This is not to say you will not be challenged: Any scrupulous rabbi you talk to will want to ascertain your sincerity to join the Jewish people, to have our back just as you are asking us to have yours, and whether you are still holding on to any prior religious commitments. But if you are sincere in your desire to take on the practices in this book (and many more besides) as essential to your identity, to forsake all other religions (but not necessarily the social and familial bonds you have with people of other religions), and cast your lot with one of the most persecuted yet most enduring and resilient peoples in the history of the world, any rabbi I know would be happy to talk to you.

Some people advocate converting through the Orthodox denomination as most "legitimate"; while all Jewish communities will accept people who converted under the instruction of Orthodox rabbis, often Orthodox Jewish communities will not accept the Jewish status of people who converted with rabbis of other denominations. These exclusive Orthodox communities are in the minority — in the U.S. at least — and every *beit din (*rabbinic court — more on that in a bit) of any denomination I've witnessed has conducted conversion rituals with the same high standards as prescribed by Jewish law in the same medieval law codes all rabbis follow for rituals like this. Like I said, every religion has its fundamentalists; we're no different. There's an old Jewish saying: "We Jews are just like everyone else, only more so."

Whether you have a rabbi to work with right away or not, the first step in the process of conversion is usually to take a class. The classes are usually called "Introduction to Judaism" or something similar, and are usually hosted by synagogues, but sometimes can be found at universities, Jewish community centers, and the like. Classes can range in schedule from 18 weeks, up to a year, or longer. My personal recommendation is that you find a class connected with the Miller Introduction to Judaism program (intro.aju.edu). The Miller program is based in Los Angeles, but its curriculum has been adopted by synagogues all over the world (it has even been translated into Spanish) and it is the best course on the subject that I have seen, and I've seen a few.

Once you take the class and get a taste of what's involved in being Jewish and joining a Jewish community, if you decide you still want to do it, you should ask a rabbi to sponsor you for conversion. You can do this even if you're still taking the class, but know for sure you want to convert when you've finished the class. The rabbi will talk you through everything that's involved, check in with you about what you've learned in your class, and help you determine whether you're ready to take the final steps: *beit din* and *mikveh*.

Beit din and *mikveh* are the last steps in converting to Judaism, and are usually scheduled for the same appointment in the same location. A *beit din* ("house of judgment" or rabbinic court) is an assembly of three rabbis convened to discuss, decide on, or witness a matter of Jewish law. Perhaps the most common reason to convene a *beit din* these days is for questioning and approving (or not) candidates for conversion to Judaism and naturalization into the Jewish people. Your rabbi can tell you more about what to expect; I wouldn't stress too much about it, because part of your sponsoring rabbi's job is to prepare you to be ready for the *beit din*, and your rabbi won't encourage you to go before the *beit din* unless he or she thinks you will be successful. Rest assured that the content of the discussion with the *beit din* is not a test on Jewish trivia designed to stump you; it is instead a conversation that allows the rabbis to ascertain whether you are sincere in your quest to join the Jewish people, of your own free will and without ulterior motive, able to set aside any prior commitment to another religion, and committed to stand with us in solidarity, as we would stand with you, come what may.

The very last step, once the rabbis of the *beit din* have approved your conversion, is to go to the *mikveh*. A *mikveh* is a gathering of water, such as the ocean, a river, or a specially designed bath that resembles a small swimming pool or a large hot tub. Most religions have some sort of ritual for spiritual cleansing or purification using water; Judaism's version is total immersion, while naked as the day you were born, in a gathering of water from a natural source (or *mayim hayim*: "living waters").

If this sounds like baptism . . . where do you think baptism came from?

The candidate for conversion immerses fully three times, saying a series of blessings in between, and when he or she emerges from the final immersion, the candidate is considered just as fully Jewish as if they were born that way, with all the rights and responsibilities of any Jew. A convert can even become a rabbi. (Wink emoji.)

A Final Promise

I began this book by making you three promises:

- I promised to teach you the very best of what I know to help you experience personal growth, meaning in your life, joy in your life, and greater human connection.
- I promised to make that teaching as accessible and effective as I can for you, regardless of your background or religion (if any).
- I promised that if you read this book, tried out the recommended actions, and reached out to me if you got stuck, you would notice change in your life for the better.

Did I keep any of these promises? Did I keep all of them?

I tried. I hope I succeeded. If I failed, I am sorry; nevertheless, I am grateful we had this time and experience of learning together. I humbly ask that if you feel like it, reach out to me and let me know how I could improve upon this work in a future edition.

But if I succeeded, I humbly ask something else: I ask you to make a promise to me.

If reading this book and putting into practice some of the ideas in this book has indeed changed your life for the better, promise me you'll share this book with someone you care about. Lend them this copy, get another copy for them, or point them to where they can find it for themselves. Just don't keep it to yourself.

I ask this not for my own ego or book sales; once more, I have no illusions about getting rich off a small-batch book about personal struggles and religion, and my closest friends will tell you, there's nothing to be done about my ego. I ask you to make this promise to me because that is a promise I made, explicitly or implicitly, to all of my teachers, without any one of whom I would not be able to teach what I have taught you. Every word I've written in the book was my way of keeping that promise, of carrying on a tradition that goes back to . . . well, all the way back.

> "Moses received the Torah from Mount Sinai and transmitted it to Joshua, and Joshua to the Elders, and the Elders to the Prophets, and the Prophets transmitted it to the Men of the Great Assembly. They said three things: Be deliberate in judgment, raise up many disciples, and make a fence for the Torah."
>
> (*Pirkei Avot* 1:1)

There have people we now call rabbis going back at least to the time that the Second Temple stood in Jerusalem, over 2,000 years ago. While in every generation rabbis have interpreted our sacred texts in ways that brought ancient traditions to bear in solving new problems, the principle goal of these rabbis has not been innovation, but rather transmission. All rabbis throughout the generations have been charged with teaching their best Torah to as many students as they could, just as Moses taught it to Joshua, and so on. Each generation, receiving the tradition, is charged with making its own judgments in interpreting the laws and traditions in ways that would best address the new challenges and new ways of living in that generation. And to be clear, the fence we are charged to make around the Torah is not for the purpose of keeping people away. Rather, it is a metaphor for creating a kind of buffer of discipline, requiring at times a higher standard of behavior than is indicated by the plain language of the text. As long as we aspire to the higher standard, we are not at risk to failing to achieve the bare minimum of the Torah's instructions.

Reader, seeker, student, friend: I want to thank you from the bottom of my heart for witnessing my transmission of the best Torah I have to teach. I sincerely hope it has helped you grow in ways you wanted, and perhaps in ways you did not expect, but still appreciate. If you have found greater meaning in your life, experienced greater joy, and formed more and better connections with other human beings, then my work with this book is done, though yours may just be beginning. For you are now a part of that tradition of the transmission of wisdom going back to a conversation between God and Moses, and then between Moses and Joshua, and so on, all the way down to me and you.

With deep gratitude for having been your teacher, I end this lesson with a question: Whom will you now teach?

GLOSSARY

Bathrobe Syndrome — Demeanor of someone with acute social deprivation or chronic loneliness, making it difficult to re-socialize. Those afflicted with this condition look like they should be wearing a bathrobe.

Beit din — (Hebrew) House of judgment, court. Refers to an assembly of at least three rabbis in order to render a legal judgment, used in the ritual for converting to Judaism.

Bli neder — (Hebrew) Without a vow. A colloquial expression usually added to a statement expressing intention in the future, such as making plans.

CE — Common Era. Refers to the current historical era on a conventional calendar; secular and non-Christian equivalent of AD ("Anno Domini" — Year of Our Lord)

I-It — A term from Martin Buber's "I and Thou" referring to an instrumental relationship, in which at least one party regards the other as an object for achieving their ends, rather than as a subject with their own ends and inherent value.

I-Thou — A term from Martin Buber's "I and Thou" referring to an appreciative relationship, in which each party recognizes the other as a subject with their own ends and inherent value.

Kabbalah — (Hebrew) Transmission, receiving. Refers to the sacred oral tradition and written literature of Jewish mysticism.

Kaddish — (Aramaic) A Jewish prayer exalting the name of God, of a heightened level of holiness that requires a minyan to recite in public. Recited by those in mourning for a close relative.

Kashrut — (Hebrew) Fitness. Refers to category of Jewish law related to ritual cleanliness or fitness for consumption, usually regarding Jewish dietary laws.

Kosher — (Hebrew) Fit, appropriate for usage or consumption.

Lashon hara — (Hebrew) Wicked tongue, evil speech. Refers to forbidden speech about another person, as explained by Rabbi Israel Meir Kagan.

Maimonides — Also known as Rabbi Moses ben Maimon, a Jewish legal scholar, philosopher, and physician of the Mediterranean region in the 12th Century CE. Author of the Mishneh Torah and other works.

Mehilah — (Hebrew) Forgiveness.

Mikveh — (Hebrew) Gathering of water. Refers to a cistern or pool of water from a natural source used for ritual cleansing by full immersion, used in the ritual for converting to Judaism.

Minyan — (Hebrew) Quorum, counting, or community. Usually refers to the gathering of at least 10 adult Jews needed to recite certain prayers in public.

Mishnah — (Hebrew) Study by repetition. Also the name of the first redaction of Oral Torah (an oral tradition of Jewish law), redacted by Rabbi Yehudah haNasi in the beginning of the 3rd Century CE.

Mishneh Torah — (Hebrew) Second Torah, Retelling of the Torah. A multi-volume code of Jewish law authored by Maimonides.

Ona'at devarim — (Hebrew) Oppressive or harmful speech. Refers to speech directed at its subject, forbidden because it is hurtful, embarrassing, or misleading.

Pirkei Avot — (Hebrew) Verses of the Ancestors, also known as the Ethics of the Fathers. A volume of Mishnah containing collected sayings of the rabbis of classical Jewish sacred literature.

Rabbi — (Hebrew) My master or my teacher. Honorific for someone ordained as a master teacher of the Torah and Jewish traditions.

Rabbi Akiva — Akiva ben Yosef. Renowned scholar who began life as an illiterate shepherd, first learned the Hebrew alphabet at age 40, became master of 48,000 students before he was executed by the Romans occupying Jerusalem in 135 CE for teaching the Torah.

Rabbi Tarfon — Torah scholar of the 1st and 2nd Centuries CE, teacher and colleague of Rabbi Akiva.

Shabbat — Weekly day of Rest ordained in the Ten Commandments, in honor of the seventh day of creation on which God rested. Observed by Jews from sundown Friday until sundown Saturday.

Shul — (Yiddish) Synagogue. Related to the German word for "school", acknowledging the synagogue's educational function within the Jewish community.

Talmud — (Hebrew) Instruction, learning. Also the name of the central work of Rabbinic literature, redacted in the 6th Century CE. Includes the Mishnah and the Gemara, a collection of commentaries on and arguments about the Mishnah, in Hebrew and Aramaic.

Tanakh — (Hebrew) The Hebrew Bible, an acronym representing the Torah, Nevi'im (Books of the Prophets), and Ketuvim (Books of the Writings).

Teshuvah — (Hebrew) Return, repentance. Refers to the Jewish practice of self-improvement, where one recognizes error, repents, makes amends with an injured party, and resolves and plans not to err in the future.

Torah — (Hebrew) Law, instruction. Could refer to: The Five Books of Moses, all books of the Jewish canon, all Jewish sacred literature, or all knowledge.

Yak shaving — Computer programming jargon for the seemingly endless series of small tasks that must be completed before the next step in a project can move forward, or a necessary task so far removed from the ultimate goal as to appear trivial.

ACKNOWLEDGEMENTS

Throughout this book, I have emphasized the value of community. I'm a strong believer in sociologist Peter Berger's principle that plausibility structures require social support. I've come to know that authors do, too, and if ever there was a plausibility structure that benefited from many hands pulling oars in one direction, it was this book, the ideas it contains, and its success in reaching your hands. I'm grateful to you for reading it, and I'm grateful to the many people who made it possible for you to read it.

First, mad props go to my Book Squad, the team of early supporters, early readers, and early adopters from many walks of my life who showed up to cheer me on as I took on the challenge of writing and publishing my first book. Squaddies, I couldn't have done it without you.

I'm indebted to my English teachers at Pomfret School: Ted Goodrich taught me to love the written word, Brad Davis taught me to love writing words, and Hagop Merjian taught me the power of words to change us.

I'm indebted to my rabbis, teachers, and mentors at the Ziegler School of Rabbinic studies: Rabbis Brad Artson, Aaron Alexander, Cheryl Peretz, Elliot Dorff, Aryeh Cohen, Shawn Fields-Meyer, Ronnie Cohen z"l, Patricia Fenton, Yehuda Hausman, Pinchas Giller, Mimi Feigelson, Dan Shevitz, Jay Strear, Richard Camras, Ed Feinstein, Avi Havivi, and Sara Berman, and professors Janet Sternfeld Davis, Ziony Zevet, Candice Levy, and Tzemah Yoreh. I'm also grateful to my teachers and rabbis at the Conservative Yeshiva in Jerusalem: Rabbis Shmuel Lewis, Gail Diamond, Mordechai Silverstein, Joel Levy, and Daniel Goldfarb, and professors Joshua Kulp and Vered Hollander-Goldfarb. All good Torah I teach I learned from them; everything good, true, and honorable in this book is theirs, but all errors and failures to hit the mark are my own.

I'm further indebted to my teachers and mentors at CLAL-The National Jewish Center for Learning and Leadership for their guidance and mentorship throughout my rabbinic education and career: Rabbis Brad Hirschfield, Irwin Kula, Rebecca Sirbu, Elan Babchuck, and Tsafi Lev. CLAL's vision of making Jewish wisdom and traditions available to all as a public good inspired me to make put my core beliefs down on the page in a form accessible to anyone they could help, and what I have learned (and the friends I have made) in the Rabbis Without Borders fellowship gave me the tools, support, motivation, cheering section, and *chutzpah* (holy audacity) to put this book into the world. To my fellow Rabbis Without Borders: You are all mutants, and I trust all of you to recognize a term of endearment, admiration, and awe when you see one.

As much as I am indebted to the those who transmitted to me the ancient tradition that has changed my life, all the more so I am indebted to the visionaries, creators, and hustlers who taught me how to transmit that tradition in an ever-changing landscape: Amy Landino, Tim Schmoyer, Roberto Blake, Gary Vaynerchuk, Casey Neistat, Simon Sinek, Timothy Ferriss, Anthony Robbins, and Seth Godin. For all your generosity in sharing your art and craft with the world, and especially to those who shared your time in gently answering all my boneheaded n00b questions, thank you.

I am deeply, deeply indebted to the leaders, volunteers, members, and my fellow *minyaneers* at Burbank Temple Emanu El, the first place that gave me my shot at teaching our traditions and building a strong and vibrant Jewish community. My rabbis taught me the Torah, but you taught me how to be a rabbi.

Big ups to all my colleagues in the rabbinate, especially Rabbi Ronald Goldberg, who taught be two things: First, where the repentant stand, saints cannot reach (*Berakhot* 34b); second, never let 'em outwork you.

Penultimately, I want to thank Kary Oberbrunner, his team at Author Academy Elite, and the whole Igniting Souls Tribe for your handiwork and inspiration in making this book a reality. You mapped the course, you called the turns, and you cheered me all the way to the finish line. You all do God's work in this world, true partners in the ongoing miracle of creation. You also connected me with an outstanding editor, Jane VanVooren Rogers, without whose encouragement, skill, sharp eye, and high standards, this book would have been a hot(ter) mess.

Last but not least: You. Yes, you. Thank you for reading this book. In the words of Seth Godin, I made this for you. I hope it changed you.

ABOUT THE AUTHOR

John Carrier found the Promised Life after a long journey from the Deep South to sunny Southern California, living all over the USA and in Israel at points in between. Born to three generations of Southern Baptist ministers but destined for another path, John was ordained as a Rabbi by the Ziegler School of Rabbinic Studies at American Jewish University in Los Angeles, California.

Before seminary, John spent eleven years consulting in financial analysis, marketing, and information systems in Washington, DC, Knoxville, and Minneapolis, in industries ranging from banking and legal services to manufacturing and microchip design. John's bread and butter in the world of commerce was translating between the Accounting Department and the IT Department, which turns out was a useful experience in translating the Torah for seekers of all spiritual backgrounds, or of no background at all.

Today John teaches about Judaism on YouTube and serves Jewish families and individuals in Burbank, California, as well as the broader community through his work with international service clubs, local interfaith partnerships, and CLAL-The National Jewish Center for Learning and Leadership, where he is a Rabbis Without Borders Fellow.

John enjoys rollercoasters, scary movies, fine dining, extreme cooking, running marathons, stepping on Legos, and marveling and the genius in his own family: his wife and two young daughters at home, and his two grown sons from afar, mostly through text messages.

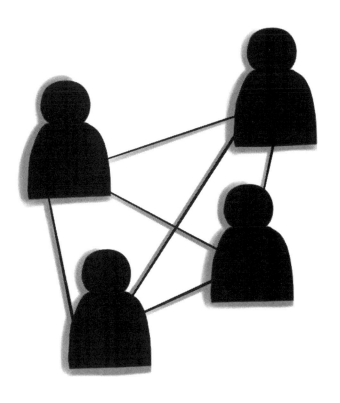

CONNECT WITH THE PROMISED LIFE TRIBE

Want to connect with others who are reading this book and putting its principles to practical use in their own lives? Need guidance on how to make the most of the Seven Gifts given your background or current situation? Connect with the Promised Life Tribe today!

Visit *www.PromisedLifeTribe.com* and sign up to get connected with:

- Additional resources to help unwrap the Seven Gifts and put them to work in transforming your life today.
- Instructions on how to connect with other Tribe members online and in your area.
- Ongoing news and updates from the Tribe.

We look forward to connecting with you, learning with you, and growing with you soon!

72380617R00117

Made in the USA
San Bernardino, CA
24 March 2018